You're born an original

don't die a copy

Other Books by John Mason

You Can Do It—Even If Others Say You Can't
Believe You Can—The Power of a Positive Attitude
An Enemy Called Average
Conquering an Enemy Called Average
Know Your Limits—Then Ignore Them
Ask . . . : Life's Most Important Answers Are Found in Asking the
Right Questions

You're born an original

don't die a copy

John Mason

Revell

a division of Baker Publishing Group
Grand Rapids, Michigan

© 1993, 2011 by John Mason

Published by Revell
a division of Baker Publishing Group
P.O. Box 6287, Grand Rapids, MI 49516-6287
www.revellbooks.com

Originally published in 1993 by Insight International.

Printed in the United States of America

Library of Congress Cataloging-in-Publication Data
Mason, John, 1955–
    You're born an original, don't die a copy / John Mason.
        p. cm.
    Originally published: Altamonte Springs, Fla. : Insight International, ©1993.
    ISBN 978-0-8007-2025-4 (pbk.)
        1. Self-acceptance—Religious aspects—Christianity. 2. Christian life.
    I. Title. II. Title: You are born an original, don't die a copy. III. Title: You are born an original, do not die a copy. IV. Title: You're born an original, do not die a copy.
    BV4647.S43M37 2011
    248.4—dc23   2011030659

Unless otherwise indicated, Scripture quotations are from the King James Version of the Bible.

Scripture quotations labeled NASB are from the New American Standard Bible®, copyright © 1960, 1962, 1963, 1968, 1971, 1972, 1973, 1975, 1977, 1995 by The Lockman Foundation. Used by permission.

Scripture quotations labeled NIV are from the Holy Bible, New International Version®. NIV®. Copyright © 1973, 1978, 1984, 2010 by Biblica, Inc.™ Used by permission of Zondervan. All rights reserved worldwide. www.zondervan.com

Scripture quotations labeled NKJV are from the New King James Version. Copyright © 1982 by Thomas Nelson, Inc. Used by permission. All rights reserved.

Scripture quotations labeled TLB are from *The Living Bible*, copyright © 1971. Used by permission of Tyndale House Publishers, Inc., Wheaton, Illinois 60189. All rights reserved.

In keeping with biblical principles of creation stewardship, Baker Publishing Group advocates the responsible use of our natural resources. As a member of the Green Press Initiative, our company uses recycled paper when possible. The text paper of this book is composed in part of post-consumer waste.

11   12   13   14   15   16   17   7   6   5   4   3   2   1

green press INITIATIVE

I am proud to dedicate this book to my wonderful wife, Linda, and our four great kids: Michelle, Greg, Mike, and Dave.

To Linda, for her prayers, agreement, and encouragement.
To Michelle, for her ideas.
To Greg, for his faith.
To Mike, for his inquisitive nature.
To Dave, for his happy spirit.

Without their love, support, and originality, this book would have never happened.

Contents

◼

Contents

Acknowledgments

It is impossible to write a book like this one without the help of some "divine connections." Special thanks to three outstanding originals:

Roger Bruhn, whose life has impacted me to be a man of character and integrity.

Mike Loomis, who has encouraged me to be an original and look to the future.

Tim Redmond, whose words always leave a positive investment in me (and who I'm honored to quote several times in this book).

Introduction

■

Years ago I worked for a very successful man, a self-made multimillionaire. Not only was he successful, he was also a very unique individual. This is something you notice quite quickly once you get to know him. It didn't take me long to see a connection between his success and his distinctiveness.

I'll never forget one day talking with him and telling him how different he was. His response at first was quite defensive: "What do you mean I'm different?" Like most people, he thought being called unique or different was negative.

Fortunately, I had a good working relationship with this boss. So I could candidly explain to him what I meant and why what I said was a good thing. I told him that his different-ness was a strong asset for him and that nearly every highly successful person I know stands out and doesn't blend it.

Well, his eyes lit up and his countenance changed the more I complimented him on his strangeness . . . in a good way.

I've always said one of the highest compliments you can hear is when someone says to you, "You're different!" You must be doing something special, matchless, and rare to hear those words.

Of course, I'm not encouraging you to be bizarre, nutty, or weird. What I am saying is as you become *you* . . . *you* will stand out. So many people are just copies.

One of the great blessings in my life is the privilege of speaking many times each year throughout the country. Because of this, I spend a fair amount of time in airports. As I walk through these terminals, I'm always moved by the hundreds of people seemingly in a hurry to nowhere. My heart goes out not only to this mass of people, but also to some specific individuals.

I wish I could stop them and ask, "Do you realize God has a unique plan for your life? Do you know that He 'packaged' you perfectly for the job? Are you aware His best for you is a life of peace, abundance, satisfaction, and love?"

That's why I wrote this book. First, to attack the mediocrity of doing anything other than what God wants you to do. Second, to stir up the gifts He's placed within you!

I know you've entrusted me with one of your most precious resources, your time. I promise to do my best to be a good steward of the minutes we spend together. That's why I organized this book into fifty-two nuggets of truth like in my first book, *An Enemy Called Average.* You won't have to wait ten pages to get one point; you'll find ten points on one page.

My prayer as you read this book is that God will reveal His plan for you, stir up what He's put inside you, and cause you to take action toward the great plan He has for your life.

PART I

Looking inward

How many outstanding generalities do you know?

■

How many outstanding people do you know with unique and distinctive characteristics? Don't be a living custard. It's true what Eric Hoffer said: "When people are free to do as they please, they usually imitate each other." Humankind is the only creation that refuses to be what it is.

Don't just look for miracles. You are a miracle. You are "fearfully and wonderfully made" (Ps. 139:14). Don't be awestruck by other people and try to copy them. Nobody can be you as efficiently and as effectively as you can. When you use the gifts you have, people call you gifted. One of the hardest things about climbing the ladder of success is getting through the crowd of copies at the bottom.

The number of people who don't take advantage of their talents is more than made up for by the number who take full advantage of the talents they have. You're a specialist . . .

an expert at what *you* do best. You're not created to be all things to all people. You're the greatest miracle in the world.

> Following the path of least resistance is what makes men and rivers crooked.
>
> Larry Bielat

More than 90 percent of all flowers have either an unpleasant odor or none at all. Yet it's the ones with fragrances we want and remember. Stand out! Too many people make cemeteries of their lives by burying their talents.

Don't try to live up to anyone's expectations but God's. A copy adapts to the world, but an original tries to make the world adapt. Therefore, all progress depends upon originals.

> Don't copy the behaviors of this world, but be a new and different person with a fresh newness in all you do and think. Then you will learn from your own experience how His ways will really satisfy you.
>
> Romans 12:2 TLB

It doesn't take a majority to make a change; it takes a few determined originals and a right cause. You're the only one in all of creation who has your set of abilities. You're special . . . you're rare. And in all rarity there is great value. Jesus says, "Let *your* light so shine before men, that they may see *your* good works" (Matt. 5:16, emphasis added). The more we're like Jesus, the more we become who we're supposed to be.

God loves you just the way you are, but He loves you too much to leave you the way you are. He wants you to use what He's put inside you. Stand out—don't blend in. Don't be a mynah bird and copy others. Leaders are like eagles: they don't flock, you find them one at a time. Be above mediocre . . . be an eagle. "Eagles commonly fly alone; the crows, daws, and starlings fly together" (John Webster).

Could *Hamlet* have been written by a committee, or the *Mona Lisa* painted by a club? Could the New Testament have been composed as a conference report? Creative ideas do not spring forth from groups. They spring from individuals. The divine spark leaps from the finger of God to the finger of Adam.

A. Whitney Griswold

While originals are always hard to find, they're easy to recognize. God leads every soul in an individual way. "There are no precedents: You are the first *you* that ever was" (Christopher Morley). There's not enough darkness in the whole world to put out the light He put in you.

🍎 You're an original.

Passion is the spark
for your fuse

■

God put inside every person the potential to be passionate. One person with passion makes a greater impact than the passive force of ninety-nine who have only interest. Too many people have "only interest" in their destiny. The book of Ecclesiastes says, "Whatsoever thy hand findeth to do, do it with thy might" (9:10). The atmosphere of your life changes dramatically when you add enthusiasm.

Everyone loves something. We're shaped and motivated by what we love. Ignore what you are passionate about and you ignore one of the greatest potentials God has put inside you. What gets your heart racing? What are you hungry to learn and know more about? What do you daydream about doing? What captures your heart and your attention?

My friend Neil Eskelin shares the following story from his outstanding book *Yes Yes Living in a No No World*:

I was attending an awards banquet of the Chase National Life Insurance Company. The speaker was the famed author of *Think and Grow Rich*, Napoleon Hill.

When Hill was introduced it was obvious his age had caught up with him. We all wondered if the octogenarian would be physically able to give the speech. (He passed away not long after this event.)

Napoleon Hill slowly walked to the podium, placed both of his hands on the sides of it, looked out at the audience and announced, "Ladies and gentlemen, I have given this speech hundreds and hundreds of times in my life. But tonight I am going to deliver it the best it has ever been given. This is going to be the best speech of my life!"

Wow! It was like a bolt of lightning. I watched 300 adults move to the edge of their chairs and absorb every word like a sponge.

Enthusiasm always makes others stand up and take notice. Nothing significant was ever achieved without enthusiasm. Jesus was a passionate man. He died for us because He loved His Father and us passionately.

Most winners are just ex-losers who got passionate. The worst bankruptcy in the world is the person who has lost his enthusiasm. When you add passion and emotion to belief, it becomes a conviction. There's a big difference between a belief and a conviction. Belief agrees with the facts. Conviction brings persistent action to your belief.

Driven by passionate conviction, you can do anything you want with your life—except give up on something you care about. Mike Murdock says, "What generates passion and zeal in you is a clue to revealing your destiny. What you love is a clue to something you contain."

Fulfilling God's plan is a passionate idea or it is nothing. There's a reason we're told to "serve the LORD thy God with all thy heart and with all thy soul" (Deut. 10:12). Henri Frederic Ameil reminds us, "Without passion man is a mere latent force and a possibility, like the flint which awaits the shock of the iron before it can give forth its spark."

You must first be a believer, then an achiever. "There are many things that will catch my eye, but there are only a very few that catch my heart . . . it is those I consider to pursue" (Tim Redmond).

🍎 **Let the passion within you rise to meet your destiny.**

Nugget #3

Questions

■

Over a million people last year bought drills. What's significant about that? Not one of those people wanted a drill. They all wanted a hole.

Questions are like drills. Answers are like holes. If you're searching for answers, you find them by drilling with the right questions.

You're where you are today because of the questions you've asked yourself. In order to get where you want to be, you have to ask yourself the right questions. The difference between successful and unsuccessful people is that successful people ask better questions and therefore get better results.

One common characteristic about successful people is that they all have the ability to ask good questions.

Quality questions = Quality life

The Bible says "Ask, and it shall be given you" (Matt. 7:7) and "Ye have not, because ye ask not" (James 4:2). What is the most common way to ask? To pose a question! The best way to *have* and *receive* is to ask questions.

Remember, it's not only the questions you ask, ~~but also the questions you fail to ask~~, that shape your destiny. Life's most important answers are found in asking the right questions.

Who said it? (an important question to ask of everything we believe) *difference?*

Do you make promises or commitments?

Do you make friends before you need them?

Does God seem far away? If so, guess who moved.

Who's creating your world?

Do you have a strong will or a strong won't?

~~The last time you failed, did you stop trying because you failed—or did you fail because you stopped trying?~~

What's it like to be my friend?

What's it like to work with me?

Are you making a living or a life?

If the future generations were dependent on you for spiritual knowledge, how much would they receive?

Do you risk enough to exercise your faith in God?

Do you say "Our Father" on Sunday and then act like an orphan the rest of the week?

Are you willing to preach what you practice?

Does failure discourage or bring determination?

Do you exist or do you live?

Is God your hope or your excuse?

How many people have made you homesick to know God?

Is your mission on earth finished?

How many happy selfish people do you know?

How many people do you know who became successful at something they hate?

What force is more potent than love?

"Is anything too hard for the LORD?" (Gen. 18:14).

If you were arrested for being kind, would there be enough evidence to convict you?

What's more miserable than being out of God's will?

🍎 **Life's most important answers are found in asking the right questions.**

Fear wants you to run from something that isn't after you

■

Fears...

The great evangelist Billy Sunday once said, "Fear knocked at my door. Faith answered . . . and there was no one there." Now, that's the proper response to fear!

Why does fear like to take the place of faith? The two have a lot in common—they both believe what you cannot see will happen. Faith ends where worry begins and worry ends where faith begins. Our worst imaginings almost never happen, and most worries die in vain anticipation.

It ain't no use putting up your umbrella till it rains.

Alice Caldwell Rice

What you fear about tomorrow is not here yet. Why be afraid of the day you've never seen?

26

Some people are so afraid to die they never begin to live.

Henry Van Dyke

It's been said, worry is a darkroom . . . where negatives are developed. Like a rocking chair, it keeps you going but you don't get anywhere. If you can't help worrying, remember that worrying can't help you either. A friend of mine once said, "Don't tell me worry doesn't do any good. I know better. The things I worry about don't happen."

A lot of people who are worrying about the future ought to be preparing for it. Fear holds you back from flexing the risk muscle. When you're robbed by worry, it's always an inside job. Worry never changes a single thing—except the worrier.

Most of our fears can be traced back to a fear of people. But the Bible says, "The LORD is the strength of my life; of whom shall I be afraid?" (Ps. 27:1).

> In God I trust and am not afraid. What can mere mortals do to me?
>
> Psalm 56:4 NIV

People would worry less about what others think of them if they only realized how seldom they do. They're not thinking about you; they're wondering what you're thinking about them!

Stop worrying about what other people are thinking. It's not what you think they're thinking. Doing this leads to doubts, then to fear, then to worry. Most people believe their doubts and doubt their beliefs. Instead, do like the old saying: "Feed your faith and watch your doubts starve to death."

Many people are so filled with fear they essentially go through life running from things that aren't after them. Fear of the future is a waste of the present.

Fear not tomorrow. God is already there. Corrie Ten Boom often said, "Never be afraid to trust an unknown future to a known God."

27

Fill up mind w/ thoughts of something... (handwritten margin note)

Follow Howard Chandler's advice. He said, "Every morning I spend fifteen minutes filling my mind full of God; and there's no room left over for worry thoughts." A famous old poem in *The Prairie Pastor* said it best:

> Said the robin to the sparrow, I should really like to know
> Why these anxious human beings rush about and worry so.
> Said the sparrow to the robin, I think it must be
> They have no Heavenly Father such as cares for you and me.

🍎 **Don't be afraid to be you.**

From this page you can go anywhere you want to

◼

Do you know what this page is noted for? This page is the springboard to your future. It's a starting point for any place in the world. You can start here and go anywhere you want to.

God has placed within each of us the potential and opportunity for success. It takes just as much effort and energy for a bad life as it does for a good life. Still, millions lead aimless lives in a prison of their own making—simply because they haven't decided what to do with their lives. It always costs more not to do God's will than to do it. In fact, "A lot of people confuse bad decision-making with destiny" (Kin Hubbard).

When you accept God's original construction for your life, you shine like a star in the night. When you choose to be a copy, you're like the darkness of the night. You can predict a person's future by their awareness of their purpose. Life's heaviest burden is to have nothing to carry. A person's significance is determined by the cause for which they live and the price they are willing to pay.

How would you like to spend two years making phone calls to people who aren't home? Sound absurd? According to one time management study, that's how much time the average person spends over a lifetime trying to return calls to people who never seem to be in. Not only that, we spend six months waiting for the traffic light to turn green and another eight months reading junk mail. These unusual statistics should cause us to "number our days" as the Bible tells us (Ps. 90:12).

unusual statistics

Don't waste one of your most precious commodities . . . time. Each minute is an irretrievable gift—an unrestorable slice of history. Realize that now is the best time to do what you're supposed to do!

What you set your heart on will determine how you spend your life. So be moved by conviction, not ego.

> Learning to praise God after the answer is obedience. Learning to praise God before the answer is faith. Obedience is good, but faith moves God.
>
> Bob Harrison

Faith builds a bridge from this world to the next. Before you can go high you must first go deep.

No wind blows in favor of a ship without a destination. A person without a purpose is like a ship without a rudder. What you set your heart on will determine how you'll spend your life. A person going nowhere can be sure of reaching that destination. Be called and sent—not up and went. God plants no yearning in your heart He doesn't plan to satisfy. Sadly, we distrust our hearts too much and our heads not enough.

Jesus, a man of purpose, once said, "To this end was I born, and for this cause came I into the world, that I should bear witness unto the truth" (John 18:37). Better to die for something than to live for nothing.

🍎 Launch out!

You're like a tea bag—not worth much till you've been through some hot water

■

Have you ever failed or made a mistake? Good, then this nugget is for you. The fact that you've failed is proof you're still a work in progress. What's more important is that you got up. Failures and mistakes can be a bridge, not a barricade, to success.

> The steps of a good man are ordered by the LORD: and he delighteth in his way. Though he fall, he shall not be utterly cast down: for the LORD upholdeth him with his hand.
>
> Psalm 37:23–24

Failure may look like a fact, but it's just an opinion. It's not how far you fall but how high you bounce that makes all the difference.

Successful people believe mistakes are just feedback. You can learn something from everything.

A teacher told her young class to ask their parents for a family story with a moral at the end of it. They were to return the next day and tell their stories.

In the classroom the next day, Joe gave his example first. "My dad is a farmer and we have chickens. One day we were taking lots of eggs to market in a basket on the front seat of the truck when we hit a big bump in the road; the basket fell off the seat and all the eggs broke. The moral of the story is not to put all your eggs in one basket."

"Very good," said the teacher.

Next, Mary said, "We are farmers too. We had twenty eggs waiting to hatch, but when they did we only got ten chicks. The moral of this story is not to count your chickens before they're hatched."

"Very good," said the teacher again, pleased with the response so far.

Next it was Barney's turn to tell his story: "My dad told me this story about my Aunt Karen. Aunt Karen was a flight engineer in the war and her plane got hit. She had to bail out over enemy territory and all she had was a bottle of whiskey, a machine gun, and a machete."

"Go on," said the teacher, intrigued.

"Aunt Karen drank the whiskey on the way down to prepare herself; then she landed right in the middle of a hundred enemy soldiers. She killed seventy of them with the machine gun until she ran out of bullets. Then she killed twenty more with the machete till the blade broke. And then she killed the last ten with her bare hands."

"Good heavens," said the horrified teacher. "What did your father say was the moral of that frightening story?"

"Stay away from Aunt Karen when she's been drinking . . ."

32

Theodore Roosevelt once said, "Far better it is to dare mighty things, to win glorious triumphs, even though checkered by failure than to rank with those poor spirits who neither enjoy much nor suffer much because they live in the great twilight that knows not victory or defeat." One of the riskiest things you can do in life is to take too many precautions and never have any failures or mistakes.

Failure is really an opportunity to start over more intelligently. No man ever achieved worthwhile success who did not at one time or other find himself teetering on the edge of disaster. If you have tried to do something and failed, you are vastly better off than if you had tried to do nothing and succeeded. The person who never makes a mistake must get awfully tired of doing nothing. If you're not making mistakes, you're not risking enough.

Vernon Sanders says, "Experience is a hard teacher because she gives the test first, the lesson afterwards." The experience of failure or mistakes will always make a person better or bitter. The choice is up to you. The good news is God has no plans that end in failure.

Edwin Louis Cole writes, "Success consists of getting up just one more time than you fell down. You don't drown by falling in the water; you drown by staying there." So get up and go on. "A man who refuses to admit his mistakes can never be successful. But if he confesses and forsakes them, he gets another chance" (Prov. 28:18 TLB).

The best way to go on is to learn the lesson and forget the details. The death of your dream will not be accomplished by a single failure. Its death will come from indifference and apathy. You must overcome mistakes and failures by finding God in the midst of them. His Word promises, "He will not fail thee, neither forsake thee: fear not, neither be dismayed" (Deut. 31:8).

Failure can become a weight or it can give you wings. The only way to make a comeback is to go on. If the truth were known, 99 percent of success is built on former failure.

A mistake proves somebody stopped talking long enough to do something. Remember the old poem by Edgar A. Guest that says, "Success is failure turned inside out."

🍎 **You have a former failure with success written all over it.**

You can't see the sunrise by looking to the west

How you position yourself to receive makes all the difference. For example, as you read this book you can begin by saying, "Lord, I will take action on what You show me." Then you will benefit more than if you just read it to be motivated or inspired. Action springs not from thought but from a readiness for responsibility. Position yourself to be ready.

I've known countless people who were excellent reservoirs of learning yet never had an outstanding idea. J. Oswald Sanders said, "Eyes that look are common. Eyes that see are rare." The problem is that we're flooded with information and starving for revelation.

To resist or receive is a decision we make every day. Nothing dies quicker than a new idea in a closed mind.

It is impossible for a man to learn what he thinks he already knows.

Epictetus

I believe Jesus responded strongly to the Pharisees because they refused to position themselves to receive.

Some people see the good, others see only the bad. Charles Francis Adams, grandson of John Adams and son of John Quincy Adams, served as a Massachusetts state senator, a US congressman, and an ambassador to Great Britain under Abraham Lincoln. He was also very conscientious about keeping a daily journal and encouraged his children to do the same.

Henry Brooks Adams, the fourth of Charles's seven children, followed his father's advice and began journaling at a young age. When he was eight, following a day spent with his father, he wrote: "Went fishing with my father today, the most glorious day of my life."

The day was so glorious, in fact, that Brooks continued to talk and write about that particular day for the next thirty years. It was then that Brooks thought to compare journal entries with his father. For that day's entry, Charles had written: "Went fishing with my son, a day wasted."

There are blessings coming to you or past you every day. Never be so stuck that you can't afford to pay attention. Availability is the greatest ability you have. The devil trembles when he hears God's weakest servant say, "I'll do what You tell me to do, Lord." When you're facing God, your back is turned away from the devil. Never give up control of your life to anything but faith.

To resist or to receive is a choice. We'll see the evidence of God everywhere or nowhere by how we position ourselves. Our walk with God begins with the command "Follow!" and ends with the command "Go!" Does God seem far away? Guess who moved. The opportunities God sends won't wake up those who are asleep.

Christians on their knees see more than the world on its tiptoes. The main problem is we won't let God help us.

Kneeling is the proper posture for putting seeds into the ground.

Brooks Atkinson

To the alert Christian, interruptions are divinely interjected opportunities. When properly viewed, every situation becomes an opportunity.

We typically see things not as they are but as we are. Too often our minds are locked on one track. We're looking for red so we overlook blue; we're thinking about tomorrow, but God's saying now; we're looking everywhere when the answer is under our nose.

Opportunities drop in your lap if you have your lap where opportunities drop. When you don't position yourself to receive, it's like praying for a bushel but only carrying a cup. When a person is positioned correctly, he or she is ready to receive all God has to give.

❦ Position yourself toward God.

Nugget #8

The person with imagination is never alone and never finished

■

Christians should be viewed not as empty bottles to be filled, but as candles to be lit. You were built for creativity. Your eyes look for opportunity, your ears listen for direction, your mind requires a challenge, and your heart longs for God's way. Your heart has eyes that the brain knows nothing of.

Make a daily demand on your creativity. Everything starts as somebody's daydream. All people of action are first dreamers. The wonder of imagination is this: it has the power to light its own fire. Ability is a flame, creativity is a fire. Originality sees things with a fresh vision. Unlike an airplane, your imagination can take off day or night in any kind of weather or circumstances. So let it fly!

First Corinthians 2:16 says, "We have the mind of Christ." Don't you know we've been given His creativity too?

A genius is someone who shoots at something no one else sees and hits it. We are told never to cross a bridge till we come to it, but this world is owned by those who have "crossed bridges" in their imaginations far ahead of the crowd. Our challenge is to consider the future and act before it occurs.

Many times we act, or fail to act, not because of will, as is so commonly believed, but because of imagination. Your dreams are an indicator of your potential greatness.

Grandmother saw Billy running around the house slapping himself and asked him why. "Well," said Billy, "I just got so tired of walking I thought I'd ride my horse for a while." One day Michelangelo saw a block of marble that the owner said was of no value. "It is valuable to me," said Michelangelo. "There is an angel imprisoned in it and I must set it free."

Other people may be smarter, better educated, or more experienced than you, but no single person has a corner on dreams, desire, or ambition. The creation of a thousand forests of opportunity can spring forth from one small acorn of an idea. As Woodrow Wilson once said, "No man that does not see visions will ever realize any high hope or undertake any high enterprise."

The Bible says, "Where there is no vision, the people perish" (Prov. 29:18). That's not God's best for you. Dissatisfaction and discouragement result not from the absence of things but from the absence of vision. Not being a person of imagination causes your life to be less than it was intended to be.

A dream is the most exciting thing there is.

🍎 Inside you there's a creative idea waiting to be released.

Decision determines destiny

My friend Bob Harrison shared this story:

> A young Egyptian girl underwent surgery to remove a second head she was born with that shared a main blood artery. This girl was born with a rare defect that occurs when an embryo begins to split into identical twins, but fails to complete the process leaving an undeveloped conjoined twin in the womb.
>
> Having two heads is not as rare a problem as many think. I've encountered many achievers that suffer from this malady. Only their problem is not in the physical arena, but in the mental arena. They are double-minded as to what is and is not really important to them and their future.

The Bible says "a double minded man is unstable in all his ways" (James 1:8). I know people who are triple- and quadruple-minded . . . I don't know what they are. It's not the difference between people that's the difficulty, it's the indifference. The fact is . . . it's a *beige* world. People are so lukewarm, medium, unsure, and uncommitted. All around us, fools seem to be growing without watering. So many people spend their lives failing and never even notice.

God wants us to be the most decisive people on the face of the earth. Why did God give us His Word and the Holy Spirit? So we can live decisive lives! How can the Lord guide someone who hasn't made up their mind which way they want to go? All of us are at fault for all of the good we *didn't* do.

> The average man does not know what to do with this life, yet wants another one which will last forever.
>
> Anatole France

The most unhappy people are those who can never make a decision. An indecisive person can never be said to belong to themselves. Don't worry about not making a decision; if you wait long enough someone else will make it for you. You can't grow while letting others make decisions for you. Indecisive people are like a blind man looking in a dark room for a black cat that isn't there.

The devil is the only one who can use a neutral person. Jesus said in Matthew 12:30, "Whoever is not with me is against me, and whoever does not gather with me scatters" (NIV). No decision *is* a decision. It doesn't require a decision to go to hell. People who demand neutrality in any situation are not really neutral but simply in favor of things not changing. Larry Bielat warns, "Mistrust the man who finds everything good, the man who finds everything evil, and still more the man who is indifferent to everything."

Meet all problems and opportunities of your life with a decision. A great deal of talent is lost for want of a little decision.

> Decision is a sharp knife that cuts clean and straight; indecision is a dull one that hacks and tears and leaves ragged edges behind.
>
> Gordon Graham

Indecision will paralyze the flow of your faith. Faith demands a decision before it can work. Every accomplishment, great or small, starts with a decision. Not every circumstance that is met can be changed, but no circumstance can be changed until it is met.

The prophet Isaiah warned Israel, "If ye will not believe, surely ye shall not be established" (7:9). And in the New Testament the apostle Paul asks, "If the trumpet give an uncertain sound, who shall prepare himself to the battle?" (1 Cor. 14:8). You will have the wrong foundation and won't know what to do if you're indecisive.

Remain indecisive, and you will never grow. To move from where you are, you must decide where you would rather be. Decision determines destiny.

❦ What is one decision you must make?

Start with what you have, not what you don't have

■

God has already given you what you need to begin creating your future. Yet most of us have found ourselves saying things like, "If I only had this . . . If only this was different . . . If only I had more money . . . then I could do what God wants me to do." And all the while we are ignoring the opportunities God has put within our reach. People always overstate the importance of things they don't have. God will never ask you for something you can't give Him. Don't know where to start? He wants you to start with what He's given you.

John Wooden, perhaps the greatest coach ever, once said, "Don't let what you cannot do keep you from doing what you can do." Prolonged idleness paralyzes initiative. To the vacillating and floundering mind everything is impossible because it *seems* so. Don't wait for extraordinary circumstances to do good; make use of ordinary situations. We don't need more strength, more ability, or greater opportunity. What we need is to use what we have, where we are.

> The lure of the distant and the difficult is deceptive. The great opportunity is where you are.
>
> John Burroughs

What you can do now is the only influence you have over your future. True greatness consists of being great in little things. Don't grumble because you don't have what you want; instead, be thankful you don't get what you deserve.

> "We must do something" is the unanimous refrain. "You begin" is the deadening reply.
>
> Walter Dwight

You *can* do everything you ought to do. Begin where you are, but don't stay where you are. People can't be happy until they've learned to use what they have and not worry over what they don't have. Happiness never comes to those who fail to appreciate what they already have. Most people make the mistake of looking too far ahead for things close by.

Make the most of what you have, no matter the circumstances, and watch God move on your behalf. Years ago, a woman received a phone call that her daughter was very sick with fever. She left work and stopped by the pharmacy for some medication for her daughter. When she returned to her car, she found she had locked the keys inside.

She had to get home to her sick daughter and didn't know what to do. She called home to talk to the babysitter and was told her daughter was getting worse. The sitter suggested, "You might find a coat hanger and use that to open the door."

The woman found an old rusty coat hanger on the ground, as if someone else had locked their keys in their car. Then she looked at the hanger and said, "I don't know how to use this."

She bowed her head and asked God for help. An old rusty car pulled up, driven by a dirty, greasy, bearded man wearing a biker skull rag on his head. The woman thought, *Great God. This is what You sent to help me?* But she was desperate, and thankful.

The man got out of his car and asked if he could help. She said, "Yes, my daughter is very sick. I must get home to her. Please, can you use this hanger to unlock my car?"

He said, "Sure." He walked over to the car and in seconds the door was opened.

She hugged the man and through her tears said, "Thank you so much. You are a very nice man."

The man replied, "Lady, I ain't a nice man. I just got out of prison for car theft."

The woman hugged the man again and cried out loud, "Thank You, God, for sending me a professional!"

The Bible tells us, "If you wait for perfect conditions, you'll never get anything done" (Eccles. 11:4 TLB). We all must row with the oars we've been given. You can never get much of anything done unless you go ahead and do it before you are ready. No one ever made a success of anything by waiting around until all the conditions were "just right."

Don't waste time in doubts and fears about what you don't have; spend yourself in the task before you, knowing the right performance of this hour's duties will be the best preparation for the hours or years that follow. As the old German proverb says, "Grow where you are planted. Begin to weave and God will give the thread."

🍎 Just do it . . . with what you have.

Destiny delayed
is the devil's delight

The most important moment in your life is right now. Don't let hesitation and procrastination keep you from your destiny. Procrastination is the symptom, fear is the problem. When you delay your duties, you delight the devil.

Be jealous of your time; it's your greatest treasure. Ideas have a short shelf life—that's why we must act before the expiration date. Procrastination is the "skill" of keeping up with yesterday.

> Even if you're on the right track—you'll get run over if you just sit there.
>
> Arthur Goodfrey

Putting off a simple thing makes it hard, and putting off a hard thing makes it impossible. Discouragement follows any decision to avoid a priority.

Obedience is God's method of provision for your life. Isaiah reminds us, "If ye be willing and obedient, ye shall eat the good of the land" (1:19). Faith triggers divine resources when you go where God leads you. Obedience brings blessings. Delayed obedience is disobedience. Obedience means "at once."

Today is the day to start. It's always too soon to stop. Many times we're not to understand, just obey. The quickest way to get out of the hole is to obey God. There's a reason God revealed the idea to you today. Peter urges, "We ought to obey God rather than men" (Acts 5:29). Choosing to obey men is what keeps us from being quick to obey God. What we all need is an alarm clock that rings when it's time to rise to the occasion.

Why don't we jump at opportunities as quickly as we jump to conclusions? Procrastination is the grave in which opportunity is buried. Anybody who brags about what he's going to do tomorrow probably did the same thing yesterday. Few things are more dangerous to a person's character than having nothing to do and plenty of time in which to do it. Killing time is not murder, it's suicide. Two things rob people of their peace of mind: work unfinished and work not yet begun.

Opportunity is often lost by deliberation. Charles Sheldon once said, "Good resolutions are like babies crying in church: They should be carried out immediately." Tackle any challenge at first sight; the longer you stare at it, the bigger it becomes. The lazier a man is, the more he's going to do tomorrow. The tragedy of life is not that it ends so soon, but that we wait so long to begin it.

The longer it takes to act on God's direction, the more unclear the direction will become. Be quick to obey, taking action without delay.

Once upon a time, the devil decided to destroy humankind. He called in all his little devils to make the plans. Anger came first and asked to be allowed to do the job by setting brother against brother. He would make people angry with each other and they would destroy themselves.

Lust also offered to go. He would defile minds and turn people into beasts by making love disappear. Next, Greed spoke and offered to destroy humankind with the most destructive of passions: uncontrolled desires. Idleness, Hate, Jealousy, and Envy each claimed in turn that they could do the job. But the devil was not satisfied with any one of them.

Finally, the last assistant came forward. He said, "I will talk with people persuasively in terms of all that God wants them to be. I shall tell them how fine their plans are to be honest, clean, and brave. I shall encourage them in the good purposes of life!"

The devil was aghast at such talk. But then the assistant continued, "I shall tell them there is no hurry. They can do all of these things tomorrow. I shall advise them to wait until conditions become more favorable before they start!" The devil replied, "You are the one who shall go to earth to destroy humankind!" The assistant's name was Procrastination.

🍎 **Kill procrastination, not time.**

There are no unimportant people

You're not insignificant. Never view your life as if Jesus did nothing for you. Make the most of yourself; that's exactly how God made you. Even a small star shines in the darkness from millions of miles away. The first and worst of all frauds is to limit oneself.

Too many people never begin what God wants them to do because they are waiting to sing like Sandi Patti, preach like Billy Graham, or write like Max Lucado. God knew what He was doing when He put you together. Use what talents *you* possess . . . the woods would be silent if the only birds singing were those that sang the best.

"All history is a record of the power of minorities, and of minorities of one" (Ralph Waldo Emerson). If you deliberately plan to be less than you're capable of being, you'll be frustrated for the rest of your life.

View others in this same light. Each person is valuable and precious. Each person knows something you don't. Learn from them. We're all created for achievement and given the seeds for greatness, but each in our own way. What is greatness? What is achievement? Doing what God wants you to do and being where He wants you to be. There are no unimportant people.

Christians are new creations, not resurfaced sinners. With God's help, you can be one of His few successes, not one of His thousands of disappointments. Don't ever forget that God calls you a friend (see John 15:13). What an incredible statement that is! He also says you're "fearfully and wonderfully made" (Ps. 139:14).

God made you special for a purpose. He has an assignment for you that no one else can do as well as you can. Out of billions of applicants for the job, you're the most qualified. You have the right combination of what it takes. God has given each person the measure of faith to do what He's called them to do. Every person is gifted.

You are never who you ought to be until you are doing what you ought to be doing. God holds us responsible not only for what we have, but for what we could have; not only for who we are, but for who we might be. People are responsible to God for becoming what God has made possible for them to become.

Your life makes a difference. Although we're all different, no mixture is insignificant. On judgment day, God won't ask me why I wasn't Joshua, Billy Graham, or Pat Robertson . . . but why I wasn't John Mason. Jerry Van Dyke said it best: "The best rose bush is not the one with the fewest thorns, but that which bears the finest roses."

🍎 You're the best person to do what God has called you to do.

Don't build a case against yourself

■

What does God think about your future? We find the answer in Jeremiah 29:11, which says, "'I know the plans I have for you,' declares the LORD, "plans to prosper you and not to harm you, plans to give you hope and a future.'" All of what we are, both good and bad, is what we have thought and believed. What you've become is the price you paid to get what you used to want.

All of the important battles we face will be waged within ourselves. Nothing great has ever been achieved except by those who dared to believe that God inside of them was superior to any circumstance. First John 4:4 says, "Greater is he that is in you, than he that is in the world."

Building a case against yourself presents thousands of reasons why you can't do what you want to, when all you really need is one reason why you can. It's a great deal better to *do* all the things you should than to spend the rest of your life wishing you had. It's been said, "Don't put water in your own boat; the storm will put enough in on its own." The first key victory you must win is over yourself. Your chief competition is *you*.

> You can't consistently perform in a manner inconsistent with the way you see yourself.
>
> Zig Ziglar

Amazingly, sometimes what you think is your greatest weakness can become a wonderful strength. Take, for example, the story of one ten-year-old boy who decided to study judo despite the fact that he had lost his left arm in a devastating car accident.

The boy began lessons with an old Japanese judo master. He was doing well, so he couldn't understand why, after three months of training, the master had taught him only one move.

"Sensei," the boy finally said, "shouldn't I be learning more moves?"

"This is the only move you know, but this is the only move you'll ever need to know," his master replied.

Not quite understanding but believing in his teacher, the boy kept training.

Several months later, the master took the boy to his first tournament.

Surprising himself, the boy easily won his first two matches. The third match proved to be more difficult, but after some time, his opponent became impatient and charged; the boy deftly used his one move to win the match.

Still amazed by his success, the boy was now in the finals.

This time, his opponent was bigger, stronger, and more experienced. For a while, the boy appeared to be overmatched. Concerned that the boy might get hurt, the referee called a time-out. He was about to stop the match when the sensei intervened.

"No," the sensei insisted. "Let him continue."

Soon after the match resumed, the boy's opponent made a critical mistake and dropped his guard. Instantly, the boy used his move to pin him. The boy had won the match and the tournament. He was the champion.

On the way home, the boy and his sensei reviewed every move from each and every match. Then the boy summoned the courage to ask what was really on his mind.

"Sensei, how did I win the tournament with only one move?"

"You won for two reasons," the teacher answered. "First, you've almost mastered one of the most difficult throws in all of judo. And second, the only known defense for that move is for your opponent to grab your left arm."

The boy's biggest weakness had become his biggest strength.

The great evangelist Dwight L. Moody said, "I've never met a man who gave me as much trouble as myself." Yes, we all relate to that. Follow the advice of my good friend Dave Blunt: "Stay out of your own way!"

Building a case against yourself is like a microscope—it magnifies trifling things but can't receive great ones. Here's a little formula to keep from building a case against yourself: multiply your prayer time, divide the truth from a lie, subtract negative influences, and add God's Word. We lie loudest when we lie to ourselves. Both faith and fear sail into the harbor of your mind, but allow only faith to drop anchor.

🍎 **Dismiss all the cases you've made against yourself.**

You can't walk backward into the future

■

It's more valuable to look where you're going than to see where you've been. Don't see your future only from yesterday's perspective. It's too easy to quantify and qualify everything and limit the dream within you.

According to Edmund Burke, "The past should be a springboard, not a hammock." You can never plan the future by the past. No one can walk backward into the future. Have you ever noticed how those for whom yesterday still looks big aren't doing much today?

Your future contains more happiness than any past you can remember. "The born-again, forgiven Christian has no past," says Tim Redmond. And Paul reminds us, "Therefore, if anyone is in Christ, the new creation has come: the old has gone, the new is here!" (2 Cor. 5:17 NIV). God doesn't consult your past to decide your future.

Misery is a yesterday person trying to get along with a tomorrow God.

Mike Murdock

Don't let your past mistakes become memorials. They should be cremated, not embalmed. It is important to look forward—your calling and destiny are there. Paul said, "Forgetting what is behind and straining toward what is ahead, I press on toward the goal to win the prize for which God has called me heavenward in Christ Jesus" (Phil. 3:13–14 NIV). You can't face your future looking backward all day long.

I like to listen to people. I specifically pay attention to the percentage of time they spend talking about the past, present, and future. I've found that those who predominately talk about the past are usually going backward. Those who talk about the present are just maintaining. But those who are talking about the future are growing. Stay away from people who only talk about the past.

Some people stay so far in the past that the future is gone before they get there. The future frightens only those who prefer living in the past. Living in the past is such an appalling waste of energy. You can't build on it.

No one has ever backed into prosperity. You can't have a better tomorrow if you are thinking about yesterday all day today. Yesterday has passed forever and is beyond our control. What lies behind us is insignificant compared to what lies ahead.

🍎 The past is past.

Go out on a limb—that's where the fruit is

■

Be bold and courageous. When you look back on your life, you'll regret the things you didn't do more than the things you did. When facing a difficult task, act as though it is impossible to fail. If you're going to climb Mount Everest, bring along the American flag. Go from looking at what you can see to believing what you can have. Don't undertake a plan unless it is distinctly important and nearly impossible. Don't bunt—aim out of the ballpark. The only limits are, as always, those of vision.

> Security is mostly a stranger. It doesn't exist in nature, nor do the children of men experience it. Avoiding danger is no safer in the long run than outright exposure. Life is either a daring adventure or nothing.
>
> Helen Keller

Mediocre people don't think of themselves as mediocre. William Winans says, "Not doing more than the average is what keeps the average down." And Ronald Osborn challenges, "Undertake something that's difficult; it will do you good. Unless you try to do something beyond what you have already mastered, you will never grow." It's difficult to say what is truly impossible, for what we take for granted today was seemingly impossible yesterday. "Impossible," Napoleon is quoted as saying, "is a word found only in the dictionary of fools." What words are found in your dictionary?

One who is afraid of doing too much always does too little. To achieve all that's possible, we must attempt the impossible. The impossible is possible! Your vision becomes your potential worth. Learn to be comfortable with great dreams.

The best jobs haven't been found. The best work hasn't been done. Christians must not stay in the shadows but stretch in the light of the cross. A person who expects nothing will never be disappointed. The only way to discover the limits of the natural is to go beyond them into the supernatural. Ask yourself, "Is anything too hard for the LORD?" (Gen. 18:14).

The readiness to take risks is our grasp of faith. William Lloyd George said, "Don't be afraid to take a big step if one is indicated; you can't cross a chasm in two small jumps." God puts no restriction on faith; faith puts no restriction on God. "But without faith it is impossible to please him" (Heb. 11:6). Your vision must be bigger than you. You should say with the psalmist, "Lead me to the rock that is higher than I" (Ps. 61:2).

"Don't avoid extremes to stay 'in balance,' stay in balance by living in the extreme God wills at that time in your life" (Tim Redmond). Unless a man takes on more than he possibly can do, he will never do all he can. Charles Spurgeon motivated his listeners by saying, "Brethren, be great believers. Little faith will bring your souls to heaven, but great faith will bring heaven to your souls."

The most disappointed people in the world are those who get just what is coming to them and no more. There are a lot of ways to become a failure, but never taking a chance is the most successful. Some things have to be believed to be seen. Attempt something so fantastic that unless God is in it it's destined for failure.

Don't bother with small plans; they motivate no one. Nothing significant was ever accomplished by a realistic person.

🍎 Your vision is your potential worth.

Be like babies . . .
they like changes

■

The late astronaut James Irwin said, "You might think going to the moon was the most scientific project ever but they literally 'threw' us in the direction of the moon. We had to adjust our course every ten minutes and we landed only inside fifty feet of our five-hundred-mile radius of our target." Life, like a trip to the moon, is full of changes and adjustments. Nothing's as permanent as change.

"When you can't change the direction of the wind—adjust your sails" (Max DePree). We can't become what we need to be by remaining what we are. When you stop changing, you stop growing. People hatc change, yet it's the only thing that brings growth.

Everyone wants to change the world, but no one thinks of changing themselves. "Poverty and shame shall be to him that refuseth instruction: but he that regardeth reproof shall be honored" (Prov. 13:18). It is a sign of strength to make changes when necessary. Not accepting the present creates a future. "Happy is the man whom God correcteth" (Job 5:17). Or as John Trapp says, "Better to be pruned to grow than cut up to burn." When God prunes us He's planning for growth.

Proverbs 13:19 says, "It is pleasant to see plans develop. That's why fools refuse to give them up even when they are wrong" (TLB). Wise people sometimes change their minds—fools, never. Be open to God's change in your plans.

The longer someone is in error, the surer they are that they're right. Defending your faults and errors only proves you have no intention of quitting them. Obstinate people do not hold opinions—opinions hold them. When people think they can't change, they stop growing.

Where we cannot invent we can at least improve. A sensational new idea is sometimes just an old idea with its sleeves rolled up. If you itch for success, keep on scratching. Everybody is in favor of progress; it's the change they don't like. Constant change is here to stay. Most people are willing to change, not because they see the light but because they feel the heat. If you're still breathing, you can improve.

Great ideas still need change, adaptation, and modification in order to prosper and succeed. Henry Ford forgot to put a reverse gear in his first automobile. Few know of his oversight. Few don't know of his success. Success and growth are unlikely if you continue to do things the way you've always done them.

❦ Change is good.

If you continue to do what's right, what's wrong and who's wrong will eventually leave your life*

I heard of a businessman who had personalized letterhead that read, "Right is right even if everyone is against it, and wrong is wrong even if everyone is for it." James 1:12 says, "Happy is the man who doesn't give in and do wrong when he is tempted, for afterward he will get as his reward the crown of life God has promised those who love Him" (TLB).

Spend less time worrying about *who's* right and take charge of deciding *what's* right in your life. Don't let someone else

* Quote attributed to David Blunt.

choose it for you. Your failures may be planned in hell, but your victory is planned by heaven. "And remember when someone wants to do wrong it is never God who is tempting him, for God never wants to do wrong and never tempts anyone else to do it" (James 1:13 TLB).

You cannot do the right thing too soon, for you never know when it will be too late. You can always find the time to do what you really want to do.

Successful people understand that no one makes it to the top in a single bound. What sets them apart is their willingness to keep putting one right step in front of the other, no matter how rough the terrain. We are what we repeatedly do. Consider the words of John Wesley:

> Do all the good you can,
> In all the ways you can,
> In all the places you can,
> At all times you can,
> To all the people you can,
> As long as ever you can.

You draw nothing out of the bank of life except what you deposit in it. The height of your potential is in proportion to your surrendering to what is right. People who live right never get left. Any act of disobedience lengthens the distance between you and your dreams. Likewise, the realization of your dreams is accomplished by sustained prayer and right action.

✹ Do what's right, then do what's right, then do what's right . . .

Failure is waiting on the path of least persistence

■

Never give up on what you know you really should do. A person with big dreams is more powerful than one with all the facts. Remember, overnight success takes about ten years. The "person of the hour" spent many days and nights getting there. Like a friend of mine once said, "My overnight success was the longest night of my life." Winners simply do what losers don't want to do longer.

Earl Nightingale tells of a young man who once asked a great and famous older man, "How can I make a name for myself in the world and become successful?" The great and famous man replied, "You have only to decide upon what it is you want and then stay with it, never deviating from your course no matter how long it takes, or how rough the road, until you have accomplished it." Success seems to be largely a matter of holding on after others have let go.

In the confrontation between the stream and the rock, the stream always wins—not through strength but perseverance. Christopher Morley said, "Big shots are only little shots that keep shooting." Endurance, patience, and commitment mean enjoying the distance between God's promises and His provision for your life. "The desire accomplished is sweet to the soul" (Prov. 13:19). Persistence may be bitter, but its fruit is sweet.

Judas, who betrayed Jesus, was an example of someone who began the good fight of faith but lacked persistence. Many of the world's great failures did not realize how close they were to success when they gave up. Stopping at third base adds no more to the score than striking out. We rate success by what people finish, not by what they start.

The secret of success is to start from scratch and keep on scratching. In his book *The Sower's Seeds*, Joel Weldon talks about the Moso, a bamboo plant that grows in China and the Far East. "After the Moso is planted, no visible growth occurs for up to five years—even under ideal conditions! Then, as if by magic, it suddenly begins growing at the rate of nearly two and one half feet per day, reaching a full height of ninety feet within six weeks! But it's not magic. The Moso's rapid growth is due to the miles of roots it develops during those first five years . . . five years of getting ready." Did this plant really grow ninety feet in six weeks or did it grow ninety feet in five years? Of course, the answer is five years. If at any time in those five years the seed had been without water, fertilizer, and nurture, the Moso plant would have died. People do not fail, they just quit too early.

God won't give up on you! Don't you give up on God. "For I am persuaded, that neither death, nor life, nor angels, nor principalities, nor powers, nor things present, nor things to come, nor height, nor depth, nor any other creature, shall be able to separate us from the love of God, which is in Christ Jesus our Lord" (Rom. 8:38–39).

Your persistence is proof you've not yet been defeated. Therefore, "Commit to the LORD whatever you do, and he will establish your plans" (Prov. 16:3 NIV). Life holds no greater wealth than steadfast commitment. It cannot be robbed from you. Only you can lose it by your lack of will.

You have no right to anything you have not pursued. For the proof of desire is in the pursuit.

Mike Murdock

The destiny of the diligent is to stand in the company of leaders. "Seest thou a man diligent in his business? He shall stand before kings" (Prov. 22:29). When faithfulness is most difficult, it's most necessary. Trying times are no time to quit trying. Enduring is a military term meaning to hold up courageously under fire. When you feel like quitting, bring more of God into that area of your life.

🍎 **Let go of whatever makes you stop.**

Nugget #19

Focus changes everything

■

In 1 Corinthians 9:25 the apostle Paul says, "To win the contest you must deny yourselves many things that would keep you from doing your best" (TLB). Doing too many things always keeps you from doing your best. The best way to bring focus into your life is to never place a question mark where God has put a period.

Don't spread yourself too thin; learn to say no positively and quickly. Focus empowers you to say no to distractions and points to the purpose of your goal. Find something in life you can lose yourself in completely.

One person with focus constitutes a majority. The person who begins too much accomplishes too little. If you wait to do a great deal of good at once, you'll never do anything. The one who is everywhere is really nowhere.

When you don't have focus, life becomes painful and confusing. "Better is a handful with quietness, than both the hands full with travail and vexation of spirit" (Eccles. 4:6).

When you don't have a good reason for doing a thing, you have one good reason for letting it alone.

We live in an age when nonessential things seem to be our only essentials. It's amazing the amount of work you can get done if you don't do anything else.

Every human mind is a great slumbering power until awakened by a keen specific desire and by definite resolution to do.

Edgar F. Roberts

Firmness of purpose is one of the most necessary ingredients of character and one of the best instruments of success. Without focus creativity wastes its efforts in a maze of inconsistencies.

The primary reason people fail is broken focus. Few things are impossible for one who is diligent and focused. God's first choice for us cannot be disorder, lack of focus, or wasting of funds or resources. Whatever you focus your attention upon, you give strength and momentum to it. Focus is the secret of strength.

Jesus said in Luke 14:33, "Whosoever of you that forsaketh not all that he hath, he cannot be my disciple." Being a disciple of Christ requires focus. When you walk with focus you will become possessed by your dreams; you'll find them expressed everywhere until you can almost smell them.

The focused straight-and-narrow way has the lowest accident rate. It's important that people know what you stand for; it's equally important that they know what you won't stand for. We can't do everything we want to do, but we can do everything God wants us to do.

❦ Focus is fantastic.

PART 2

Looking outward

Leave everyone better than you found them

∎

Proverbs 11:24–25 says, "It is possible to give away and become richer! It is also possible to hold on too tightly and lose everything. Yes, the liberal man shall be rich! By watering others, he waters himself" (TLB). You were created to help others.

Those who are best at helping others are always able to see the bright side of other people's troubles. Practicing the Golden Rule is not a sacrifice, it's an investment. Don't give until it hurts, give until it feels good.

What we do for ourselves alone dies with us; what we do for others lives beyond us. An old epitaph reads, "What I gave, I have. What I spent, I had. What I kept, I lost." No person is more deceived than the selfish person.

No man was ever honored for what he received. Honor has been the reward for what he gave.

Calvin Coolidge

Invest in the success of others. When you help someone up a mountain, you'll find yourself close to the summit too.

If you want others to improve, let them hear the nice things you say about them. People will treat you the way you view them. Find the good in everyone. To lead people, make them feel you are behind them. Most people can live for two months on five words of praise and a pat on the back.

The good things you make happen for others, God will make happen for you. "Knowing that whatsoever good thing any man doeth, the same shall he receive of the Lord" (Eph. 6:8). You grow spiritually to the extent you give out. By giving out, you create room to grow on the inside.

"Give instruction to a wise man, and he will be yet wiser: teach a just man, and he will increase in learning" (Prov. 9:9). You may be the only Bible some people will ever read. As D. L. Moody once said, "Where one reads the Bible, a hundred read you and me."

What means most in life is what you've done for others. The best way to encourage yourself is to try to encourage somebody else. It's the duty of all Christians to make it difficult for others to do wrong, easy to do right.

> Those who bring sunshine to the lives of others cannot keep it from themselves.
>
> J. M. Barrie

After people have been around you, do they feel better or worse? Bigger or smaller? Full of faith or fear? Are you leaving people better than you found them?

If you treat people as they are, they will remain as they are. If you treat them as though they were what they could be, you'll help them become what they could be. There's no better exercise for the heart than reaching down and lifting someone else up.

🍎 **Find someone to help.**

Don't spend your life standing at the complaint counter

■

The person who's always finding fault seldom finds anything else. So live your life as an exclamation, not an explanation. Any complainer will tell you success is nothing but luck.

Children are born optimists. They laugh more than a hundred times a day, adults less than five. They expect the best.

A pastor was giving the children's message during church. For this part of the service, he would gather all the children around him and give a brief lesson before dismissing them for children's church.

On this particular Sunday, he was using squirrels for an object lesson on industry and preparation. He started out by saying, "I'm going to describe something, and I want you to raise your hand when you know what it is." The children nodded eagerly. "This thing lives in trees (pause) and eats nuts (pause) . . ." No hands went up.

"And it is gray (pause) and has a long bushy tail (pause) . . ." The children were looking at each other, but still no hands rose. "And it jumps from branch to branch (pause) and chatters and flips its tail when it's excited (pause) . . ."

Finally one little boy tentatively raised his hand. The pastor breathed a sigh of relief and called on him. "Well," said the boy, "I *know* the answer must be Jesus . . . but it sure sounds like a squirrel to me!"

Look for the best. The more you complain, the less you'll obtain. A life of complaining is the ultimate rut. The only difference between a rut and a grave is their timing. A complaining spirit is first a caller, then a guest, and finally a master.

Some people always find the bad in a situation. Do you know people like that? How many successful complainers do you know?

> Little men with little minds and little imagination go through life in little ruts, smugly resisting all changes which would jar their little worlds.
>
> Anonymous

Small things affect small minds. Some people are confident they could move mountains if only someone else would clear the rocks out of their way. Some of the most disappointed people in the world are those who get what is coming to them.

Misery wants your company but you don't have to join in. Complainers attract other complainers while repelling positive people. When God gets ready to bless you, He doesn't send complainers into your life. He sends those full of faith, power, and love.

When you feel like complaining, bring God into the situation. You have shut out His light to be in the dark. "Thou wilt keep him in perfect peace whose mind is stayed on thee" (Isa. 26:3). Are you waiting on God, or is He waiting on you? Is God your hope or your excuse? Is He your friend or foe? Don't let heaven become a complaint counter.

Of all sad words of tongue or pen,
The saddest are these:
"It might have been!"
John Greenleaf Whittier

Don't complain. The wheel that squeaks the loudest often gets replaced. If you're busy complaining about other people, you won't have time to love them.

❦ When you complain, you explain your pain for no gain.

If you're green with envy, you're ripe for problems

■

One of the most valuable decisions we can make is to not let our own lives be influenced by what's happening in other people's lives. What happens in someone else's life has nothing to do with what God wants to do in yours. He loves you just as much as He loves others, for the Bible tells us that "God is no respecter of persons" (Acts 10:34). Every time we put our eyes on other people, we take our eyes off God. Jesus asks, "Why beholdest thou the mote that is in thy brother's eye, but considerest not the beam that is in thine own eye?" (Matt. 7:3).

Some people seem to know how to live everybody's lives but their own. Envy is the consuming desire to have everybody else a little less successful than you are. Don't measure your life by what others have or haven't done. Remember that "love does not envy" (1 Cor. 13:4 NKJV). Jealousy is the tribute mediocrity pays to achievers. Criticizing another's garden doesn't keep the weeds out of your own.

Great minds discuss ideas, average minds discuss events, and small minds discuss people.

Dr. Laurence J. Peter

Envy is a tremendous waste of mental energy. Refrain from envy—it's the source of most unhappiness. If you're comparing yourself with others, that view is distorted. Most of us measure our success by what others haven't done. Don't let others set your limits, for when they do it's always too low. Winston Churchill once said, "Don't be content to be the chip off the old block; be the old block itself." "Don't be a fraction, be a whole" (Greg Mason).

People who are envious are always quick to find the negative. There once was a hunter who came into possession of a special bird dog. The dog was the only one of its kind, because it could walk on water. One day he invited a friend to go hunting with him so that he could show off his prized possession.

After some time, they shot a few ducks, which fell into the river. The man ordered his dog to run and fetch the birds. So the dog ran on the water to fetch them. The man was expecting a compliment about the amazing dog, but he did not receive it.

Being curious, the man asked his friend if he had noticed anything unusual about the dog. The friend replied, "Yes, I did see something unusual about your dog. Your dog can't swim!"

Most of the people we face every day are negative. They choose to look at the hole in the middle rather than the doughnut. Do not expect compliments or encouragement from them. These are the people who cannot pull you out of your present situation. They can only push you down.

So be aware of them, spend less time with them, and do not let them steal your dreams away from you.

Don't surrender leadership of your destiny to outside forces. George Craig Stewart says, "Weak men are the slaves of what happens. Strong men are masters of what happens." The shoe doesn't tell the foot how big to get. Having the right perspective propels you to act from vision and not from others' circumstances. The *copy* competes against others; an *original* competes against himself.

People are foolish creatures who try to get even with enemies and get ahead of friends. Love looks through a telescope; envy looks through a microscope. There are many roads to hate, but envy is one of the shortest of them all. We underrate or exaggerate what we don't possess. Don't envy anybody. You have something no other person has. Develop it and make it outstanding.

Tim Redmond says, "A leader is one of many accomplishments. What sets him apart from others is he is not swayed by opposition or praise or comparison." God enters by a private door into every individual. He leads each of us by a separate path. No one can build their destiny on the success of another person. What the small person seeks is in others; what the superior person seeks is in God.

🍎 **The only way to see is to keep your eyes on God.**

The sky's not the limit

No one can put a limit on you without your permission. It was because of their attitudes—not the giants—that the Israelites didn't enter the Promised Land.

Eli Whitney was laughed at when he showed his cotton gin. Edison had to install his electric light free of charge in an office building before anyone would even look at it. The first sewing machine was smashed to pieces by a Boston mob. People scoffed at the idea of railroads. People thought traveling thirty miles an hour would stop the circulation of the blood. Morse had to plead before ten Congresses before they would even look at his telegraph. Yet for all these men the sky was not the limit.

> Beware of those who stand aloof
> And greet each venture with reproof.
> The world would stop if things were run
> By men who say "It can't be done."
> Anonymous

Jesus tells us, "Seek, and ye shall find" (Matt. 7:7). We attain only in proportion to what we attempt. More people are persuaded to believe in nothing than to believe in too much. As Jesus told the blind men, "According to your faith be it unto you" (Matt. 9:29). You are never as far from the answer as it first appears. It's never safe or accurate to look into the future without faith.

So how can you find? You must seek. Tell me what you believe about Jesus and I can tell some important facts about your future. What picture of Jesus do you have? Was He merely a good man with good ideas? Or is He the Son of the living God, our advocate before the Father, the King of Kings and Lord of Lords?

Be more concerned about what the still small voice whispers than about what other people shout. A lot of people no longer hope for the best, they just hope to avoid the worst. Many of us have heard opportunity knocking at our door, but by the time we unhooked the chain, pushed back the bolt, turned two locks, and shut off the burglar alarm—it was gone! Too many people spend their lives looking around, looking down, or looking behind. God says, *Look up*. The sky's not the limit.

🍎 The sky's not the limit.

Face the music, and someday you will lead the band

■

Not all obstacles are bad. In fact, an opportunity's favorite disguise is an obstacle. Conflict is simply meeting an obstacle on the road to your answer. The fight is good; it's proof you haven't quit. The apostle Paul said it best when he wrote, "We are pressed on every side by troubles, but not crushed and broken. We are perplexed because we don't know why things happen as they do, but we don't give up and quit. We are hunted down, but God never abandons us. We get knocked down, but we get up again and keep going" (2 Cor. 4:8–9 TLB).

Being a Christian doesn't remove you from the world and its problems; rather, it equips you to live productively and victoriously in the world. No one is immune to problems. The lion has to defend itself against flies. If you want your place in the sun, you'll have to expect some blisters.

Growth and success don't eliminate obstacles; they create new ones. God is always working on us and walking with us. Thomas Carlisle said, "The block of granite which was an obstacle in the pathway of the weak becomes a stepping-stone in the pathway of the strong."

Bringing a giraffe into the world is a tall order. A baby giraffe falls ten feet from its mother's womb and usually lands on its back. Within seconds it rolls over and tucks its legs under its body. From this position it considers the world for the first time as it shakes off the last vestiges of birthing fluid from its eyes and ears. Then the mother giraffe rudely introduces her offspring to the reality of life. How? By kicking the calf head over heels repeatedly until the calf rises to its feet for the first time.

The calf benefits from this harsh treatment by learning to move quickly around predators. This keeps the calf safe.

We need to change the way we view obstacles. In the midst of trials, God wants growth and promotion for you. Trials provide an opportunity to grow, *not* die. Obstacles can temporarily detour you, but only you can stop. All obstacles reveal what you really believe and who you really are. They introduce you to yourself.

Your struggle may be lasting but it is not everlasting. The devil wants you to think there's nothing more permanent than your temporary situation. It's the struggle that makes you strong, because you grow through adversity, not pleasure.

As I've traveled, I've noticed that no matter how cloudy it is when the plane takes off, above the clouds the sun always shines. Look up! It's not the outlook but the *uplook* that counts. Obstacles are a part of life.

Jesus said, "In the world ye shall have tribulation: but be of good cheer; I have overcome the world" (John 16:33). Jesus doesn't say, "There is no storm." He says, "I am here; do not tremble, only trust." The difference between iron and steel is fire. God never promised it would be easy. However, He did say that "all things are possible to him that believeth" (Mark 9:23).

> In the presence of trouble, some people grow wings; others buy crutches.
>
> Harold W. Ruoff

Adversity not only changes people; it also unmasks them. As Studs Terkel said, "Face the music, and someday you will lead the band." When God's at our side He helps us to face the music, even when we don't like the tune. Don't just look to God through your circumstances; look at your circumstances through God.

🍎 **Your problem is your promotion.**

Nugget #25

You're created to be an answer

■

Basketball coach John Wooden said, "You cannot live a perfect day without doing something for someone who will never be able to repay you." I believe a powerful verse in the Bible that releases the blessing of God in your life is Proverbs 3:27, which says, "Withhold not good from them to whom it is due, when it is in the power of thine hand to do it." I can't tell you how many times it's been a joy to help someone in this way. I love it when they ask, "Why did you do this?" and I'm humbled to say, "Because I can . . ."

Joy shared is joy doubled. You're created to be a part of the solution. Helen Keller once said, "I am only one; but still I am one. I cannot do everything, but still I can do something; I will not refuse to do the something I can do."

Be an answer. Get in the way if someone you know is on their way down. Walk in when others are walking out.

There are no unimportant jobs, no unimportant people, and no unimportant acts of kindness. If you haven't got any kindness in your heart, you have the worst kind of heart trouble.

Be nice—you never know the good it will do or the bad it will prevent. Next time a sales clerk looks down her nose at you, remember the story of millionaire John Barrier and the Washington state bank that refused to validate his parking.

John Barrier had done business with Old National Bank (now U.S. Bank) in Spokane, Washington, for thirty years. He'd made his money buying and refurbishing old buildings, and he was wearing his usual shabby clothes one day in October 1988 when he left his pickup truck in a nearby parking lot while he paid a visit to his broker, then cashed a check at the bank. The bank teller, however, took one look at his grubby clothes and refused to stamp the parking bill.

He said, "If you have $1 in a bank or $1 million, I think they owe you the courtesy of stamping your parking ticket." John Barrier withdrew all his money from the bank and took it to another bank down the street.

Your contribution is determined by the answers you give to the problems you face. According to Mike Murdock, "You'll only be remembered for two things: the problems you solve or the ones you create." It's always more blessed to give than to receive (see Acts 20:35).

Give of yourself to others and watch criticism, depression, and unhappiness leave your life. Critics are usually the most inactive of people. Walk in your neighbor's shoes, sit in your boss's chair, walk the path of your best friends. Be on the lookout for ways to be an answer.

How many happy selfish people do you know? You can make more friends in two months by helping other people than you can in two years by trying to get others to help you. "If God can get it through you, He will give it to you," says Pastor E. V. Hill.

The Dead Sea is a dead sea because it continually receives and never gives.

Anonymous

Just one act of yours may be all it takes to turn the tide of another person's life. Find the problems you're an answer to.

🍎 What's in the power of your hand to do?

Words are like nitroglycerine— they can blow up bridges or heal hearts

■

Just to see how it feels, refrain from saying anything bad about anybody or anything for the next twenty-four hours. Mark Twain is famous for saying, "The difference between the right word and the almost right word is the difference between lightning and the lightning bug." "Idle hands are the devil's workshop, idle lips are his mouthpiece" (Prov. 16:27 TLB). What the writer of Proverbs says is true: "Death and life are in the power of the tongue" (Prov. 18:21).

You can tell more about a person by what he says about others than you can by what others say about him. Out of the abundance of the heart the mouth speaks (Jesus, Matt. 12:34). An original person says, "Let's find a way." A copy says, "There is no way." The original says, "There should be a better way to do it." A copy says, "That's the way it's always been done here." Instead of using the words "if only," try substituting "next time." Don't ask, "What if it doesn't work?" Instead, say, "What if it does?"

Ignorance is always eager to speak. The best time for you to hold your tongue is the time you feel you *must* say something or bust. Not even the fastest car can catch a word spoken in anger. You'll never be hurt by anything you didn't say. Silence is the ultimate weapon of power; it's also one of the hardest arguments to dispute. It's a mistake to judge a person's horsepower by their exhaust. Some people speak from experience; others, from experience, don't speak.

Take a tip from nature—your ears weren't made to shut, but your mouth was! When an argument flares up, a wise person quenches it with silence. Sometimes you have to be quiet to be heard. It's when the fish opens its mouth that it gets caught.

Your words are a reflection of where you're going. Jesus said, "Your words now reflect your fate then: either you will be justified by them or you will be condemned" (Matt. 12:37 TLB).

A group of frogs were traveling through the woods, and two of them fell into a deep pit. All the other frogs gathered around the pit. When they saw how deep the pit was, they told the two frogs that they were as good as dead.

The two frogs ignored the comments and tried to jump out of the pit with all of their might. The other frogs kept telling them to stop, that they were as good as dead. Finally, one of the frogs took heed to what the other frogs were saying and gave up. He fell down and died.

The other frog continued to jump as hard as he could. Once again, the crowd of frogs yelled at him to stop the pain and just die. He jumped even harder and finally made it out. When he got out, the other frogs said, "Did you not hear us?" The frog explained to them that he was deaf. He thought they were encouraging him the entire time.

This story reveals a valuable lesson: the tongue can be both helpful and hurtful. An encouraging word to someone can lift them up and help them make it. A destructive word to someone can be what it takes to put them down and stop them.

Hopeful words can go such a long way. Anyone can speak words that rob another of the spirit to continue in difficult circumstances.

"Now go ahead and do as I tell you, for I will help you to speak well, and I will tell you what to say" (Exod. 4:12 TLB). When you don't know what to say, ask God and He will help you. In order to know people, listen carefully when they mention their dislikes. Flapping your gums dulls your two most important senses—your eyes and ears. Many a good relationship has been smothered to death by wrong words and misunderstood words.

Words have consequences. Words are seeds that always bring a harvest. So use them wisely.

> A wise old owl sat on an oak,
> The more he saw the less he spoke;
> The less he spoke the more he heard;
> Why aren't we like that wise old bird?
> Edward H. Richards

 Watch your words.

Nugget #27

Unforgiveness has no foresight

■

There's one guaranteed formula for choking off originality inside each of us—unforgiveness. "Never cut what can be untied" (Joseph Joubert). When you have been wronged, a poor memory is your best response. Never carry a grudge: while you're straining under its weight, the other guy's out producing. One of the most lasting pleasures you can experience is the feeling that comes over you when you genuinely forgive an adversary . . . whether they know it or not.

Forgive your enemies—nothing will annoy them more. There's no revenge as sweet as forgiveness. The only people you should try to get even with are those who have helped you.

Henry Ward Beecher once said, "Forgiveness ought to be like a canceled note—torn in two, and burned up, so it never can be shown against one." Never is God operating in your life as strongly as when you forego revenge and dare to forgive an injury. "He who cannot forgive, destroys the bridge over which he may one day need to pass" (Larry Bielat). Hate, bitterness, and revenge are luxuries you cannot afford.

Forgiveness heals; unforgiveness wounds. Be quick to forgive. People need to be loved the most when they deserve it the least. Jesus urges, "Come to terms quickly with your enemy before it is too late" (Matt. 5:25 TLB). The best healing is quick healing.

You can't get ahead when you're trying to get even. Don't be offended; being offended is a strategy of Satan to get you out of the will of God. When we think about an offense, trouble grows; when we think about God, trouble goes.

When you don't forgive, you're ignoring how that impacts your destiny. How much more grievous are the consequences of unforgiveness than the causes of it! Douglas Steere warns, "Hate is a prolonged form of suicide." There's nothing more pathetic than a person who has harbored a grudge for many, many years.

It's true . . . the one who forgives, ends the quarrel. Patting a person on the back is the best way to get a chip off their shoulder. Forgive your enemies—you can't get back at them any other way! Forgiveness saves the expense of anger, the high cost of hatred, and the waste of energy.

There are two marks of a Christian: giving and forgiving. Hate is the most inefficient use you can make of your mind. If you want to be miserable, hate somebody. Hatred does a great deal more damage to the vessel in which it is stored than the object on which it is poured.

Norman Cousins once wrote, "Life is an adventure in forgiveness." Every person should have a special cemetery lot in which to bury the faults of friends and loved ones. "To forgive is to set a prisoner free and discover the prisoner was you" (anonymous).

● **Forgive someone every day.**

What good is aim if you don't know when to pull the trigger?

■

God is a God of timing *and* direction. He wants us to know what to do and when to do it. In Psalm 32:8 He promises, "I will instruct thee and teach thee in the way which thou shalt go: I will guide thee with mine eye." Don't live your life ahead or outside of His will.

Patience will do wonders, but it wasn't much help to the man who planted an orange grove in Alaska. There's never a right time to do the wrong thing. If you take too long in deciding what to do with your life, you'll find you've lived it. Time was invented by almighty God in order to give dreams a chance. "Hell is truth seen too late—duty neglected in its season" (Tryon Edwards). Ideas won't keep . . . something must be done about them.

> There is one thing stronger than all the armies in the world, and that is an idea whose time has come.
>
> Victor Hugo

One cool judgment is worth a thousand hasty judgments. When Billy Graham got off an airplane one day, there was a limousine waiting for him. Even though he was over ninety years old, he walked up to the limousine driver and said, "You know what, I've never driven a limousine before. I want to drive the limousine."

The driver said, "Okay, I'll let you drive it." So Billy Graham got into the limousine and started driving. He wasn't used to driving a limousine, and soon was going 70 miles an hour in a 55-mile-an-hour zone. A rookie policeman pulled him over, walked up to the car, looked in, and saw Dr. Billy Graham. The policeman was a little nervous as he said, "May I see your license, sir?" He looked at the license, and sure enough—it was Dr. Billy Graham.

The rookie walked back to his squad car, called headquarters, and said, "Look, I have just stopped a very, very important individual."

"How important is he?" came the reply from headquarters.

"Well, he's very important."

"Is he more important than the governor?"

"He's more important than the governor."

"Is it the president of the United States?"

"He's more important than the president of the United States."

"Well, who is it?"

"Well, I think it's the Lord because Billy Graham is his chauffeur."

Jumping to a wrong decision seldom leads to a happy landing. Too many people leave the right opportunity to look for other opportunities. Seize today's opportunities today and tomorrow's opportunities tomorrow.

Always apply light, not heat, to your dreams. God teaches us that His Word is a lamp unto our feet and a light unto our path (see Ps. 119:105). The lamp illuminates things we are dealing with close at hand. The light on our path enlightens our future direction.

Don't hurry when success depends on accuracy. Those who make the worst use of their time are the first to complain of its shortness. The fastest running back is useless unless heading toward the right goal line.

Timing is the vital ingredient for success. "For the vision is yet for an appointed time" (Hab. 2:3). There is an appointed time for your vision. Have 20/20 vision. Don't be too farsighted or too nearsighted. As I've studied godly leaders, I've found at key times they have said, "God lead me to do . . . " Obedience to God's will is the GPS on the road of His plan for you.

Following His perfect will releases the originality within you and helps you identify priorities. If Jesus is the Way, why waste time traveling some other way?

🍎 **Ask God for His timing and direction.**

Today I will . . .

■

Rise early because no day is long enough for a day's work.

Compliment three people.

Make myself valuable to somebody.

Not lose an hour in the morning and spend all day looking for it.

Tackle a problem bigger than me.

Have a small improvement in some area.

Go from thinking TGIF to TGIT—thank God it's today.

Take three actions outside my comfort zone.

Know the devil hates this new day because I'm up again.

Die to myself.

Give thanks for my daily bread.

Leave someone a little better than I found them.

Be aware the earth praises the Lord.

Give my best time of the day to communion with God.

Find something to do differently.

Live by the Golden Rule so I'll never have to apologize for my actions tomorrow.

Know the place to be happy is here, the time to be happy is now.

Take small steps to conquer a bad habit.

Judge this day not by the harvest, but by the seeds I plant.

What you do every day really matters. There's a reason God makes each day twenty-four hours long and then starts it all over again the next day.

My favorite thing to say before my feet hit the floor at the start of every day is, "This is the day that You made, Lord. I will rejoice and be glad in it. Let the words of my mouth and the meditations of my heart be acceptable to You, my strength and my redeemer. Let everything I say and do bring glory to You. Now, Lord, I need all the help I can get!"

🍎 **The secret to your success is hidden in your daily routine.**

You're created for connection

God didn't write solo parts for us. He has divine connections for you—right friends and associations. These good relationships always bring out the original in you. You know the kind of people I'm talking about; after you've been with them you find yourself less critical, full of faith, and having a vision for the future. So respect those God has assigned to help you. The worth of any relationship can by measured by its contribution to your vision, plan, or purpose. Someone is always observing you who is capable of greatly blessing you.

It's very important who we closely associate with. Have you ever known a backslider who didn't first hang around with the wrong kind of people? The devil doesn't use strangers to deter or stop you. These wrong associations bring out the worst in you, not the best. After you're around them you'll find yourself full of doubt, fear, confusion, and criticism. The devil's favorite entry into your life is usually through those you are closest to.

As you grow in God, your associations will change. Some of your friends won't want you to grow. They'll want you to stay where they are. Friends who don't help you climb will want you to crawl. Your friends will either stretch your vision or choke your dream.

Never let anyone talk you out of pursuing a God-given idea. "Don't let someone else create your world for you, for when they do they always make it too small" (Ed Cole). Who's creating your world?

Never receive counsel from unproductive people. Never discuss your problems with someone incapable of contributing to the solution. Those who never succeed themselves are always first to tell you how.

Not everyone has a right to speak into your life.

Once upon a time, a beautiful, independent, self-assured princess happened upon a frog in a pond. The frog said to the princess, "I was once a handsome prince until an evil witch put a spell on me. One kiss from you and I will turn back into a prince. Then we can marry and move into the castle with my mom. You can prepare my meals, clean my clothes, bear my children, and forever feel happy doing so."

Later that night, while the princess dined on frog legs, she kept laughing and saying, "I don't think so!" Remember, not everyone has a right to speak into your life . . . so stop letting them.

You are certain to get the worst of the bargain when you exchange ideas with the wrong person. I like to put it this way: don't follow anyone who's not going anywhere. We are to follow no person farther than he or she follows Jesus.

Mike Murdock says, "When God gets ready to bless you, He brings a person into your life." God cares for people through people.

With some people you spend an evening; with others you invest it. Be careful where you stop to inquire for directions along the road of your life. Wise is the person who fortifies life with the right friendships.

🍎 You become like those you closely associate with.

When others throw bricks at you, turn them into stepping-stones

All great ideas create conflict, battle, and wars. In other words, your destiny creates challenges and criticism.

Every great, big, and unique idea has three stages of responses:

- "It's impossible—don't waste the time and the money."
- "It's possible but has a limited value."
- "I said it was a good idea all along."

Our response to critics should be what Paul says: "We are perplexed, but not in despair; persecuted, but not forsaken; cast down, but not destroyed" (2 Cor. 4:8–9). Love your enemies, but if you really want to make them mad, ignore them completely.

Criticism of Christians is the language of the devil. The Bible describes the devil as the accuser of the brethren. Therefore, we should consider Jesus's words: "He that is without sin among you, let him cast the first stone" (John 8:7). Bees can't make honey and sting at the same time. Attention men: before you criticize another, look closely at your sister's brother!

We should heed the still small voice, not the deafening blasts of doom. If your head sticks up above the crowd, expect more criticism than bouquets. Satan always attacks those who can hurt him the most. God works from the inside out; the devil tries to work from the outside in.

Whoever criticizes *to* you will criticize *about* you. A person who belittles you is only trying to cut you down to his or her size. A critic is one who finds fault without a search warrant. A statue has never been set up to a critic.

A bus carrying only ugly people crashes into an oncoming truck, and everyone inside dies. As they stand at the pearly gates waiting to enter paradise and meet their maker, God decides to grant each person one wish because of the grief they have experienced.

They're all lined up, and God asks the first person to make a wish. "I want to be gorgeous," and so God snaps His fingers and it is done.

The second one in line hears this and says, "I want to be gorgeous too." Another snap of God's fingers and the wish is granted.

This goes on for a while, with each one asking to be gorgeous. But when God is halfway down the line, the last guy in the line starts laughing. When there are only ten people left, this guy is rolling on the floor, laughing his head off.

Finally, God reaches this last guy and asks him what his wish will be. The guy eventually calms down and says, "Make 'em all ugly again."

You can always tell a failure by the way he or she criticizes success. Failures never offer a better solution to a problem. Those who can—do. Those who can't—criticize. Those who complain about the way the ball bounces are often the ones who dropped it. If it weren't for the doers, the critics would soon be out of business. Envy provides the mud that failures throw at success. Those who are throwing mud are simultaneously losing mud. Small minds are the first to criticize large ideas.

If people talk negatively about you, live so no one will believe them. Fear of criticism is the kiss of death in the courtship of achievement. If you're afraid of criticism, you'll die doing nothing. A successful person is someone who can lay a firm foundation with the bricks others throw at them.

🍎 **Criticism is a compliment when you're following God's plan.**

There's no such thing as a self-made man

■

No one can make it alone. Remember, if you try to go it alone, the fence that shuts others out also shuts you in. "God sends no one away except those who are full of themselves" (D. L. Moody). The person who only works by themselves and for themselves is likely to be corrupted by the company they keep.

There is no such thing as a "self-made" man or woman. We are made up of thousands of others.

> Everyone who has ever done a kind deed for us or spoken one word of encouragement to us has entered into the make-up of our character and of our thoughts, as well as our success.
>
> George Matthew Adams

Have a grateful heart and be quick to acknowledge those who help you. Make yourself indispensible to somebody. It's easy to blame others for your failures, but do you credit others with your successes?

"Tunnel vision tells you nobody is working as hard as you are. Tunnel vision is an enemy of teamwork. It's a door through which division and strife enter" (Tim Redmond). Few burdens are heavy when everybody lifts. Freckles would make a nice coat of tan if they would get together.

Everyone needs someone. An elderly couple walked into a fast food restaurant. The little old man walked up to the counter, ordered the food, paid, and took the tray back to the table where the little old lady sat. On the tray was a hamburger, a small bag of fries, and a drink.

Carefully, the old man cut the hamburger in two and divided the fries into two neat piles. He sipped the drink and passed it to the little old lady, who took a sip and passed it back.

A young man at a nearby table had watched the old couple and felt sorry for them. He offered to buy them another meal, but the old man politely declined, saying that they were used to sharing everything. The old man began to eat his food, but his wife sat still, not eating.

The young man continued to watch the couple. He still felt he should be offering to help. As the little old man finished eating, the old lady had still not started on her food. "Ma'am, why aren't you eating?" asked the young man sympathetically.

The old lady looked up and said politely, "I'm waiting for the teeth." We all need help from someone . . .

If you believe in nothing but yourself, you live in a very small world—one in which few will want to enter. The one who sings one's own praises may have the right tune but the wrong words. Conceited people never get anywhere because they think they're already there.

Every great person is always being helped by somebody. The higher you go in life, the more dependent you will become on other people. Woodrow Wilson was quoted as saying, "I not only use all the brains I have, but all that I can borrow." Behind a capable person there are always other capable people.

Work together with others. Remember the banana—every time it leaves the bunch, it gets peeled and eaten. You'll never experience lasting success without relationships. No one person alone can match the cooperative effort of the right team.

🍎 Find someone who can help you.

A smile is mightier than a grin

■

The most bankrupt person in the world is one who has lost joy. Every great and commanding movement in the history of the world incorporated enthusiasm. Nothing great was or will be achieved without it. So decide to become the most positive and enthusiastic person you know.

In a recent survey, two hundred national leaders were asked what makes a person successful. Eighty percent listed enthusiasm as the most important quality. Some pursue happiness—others create it. A person who is enthusiastic soon has enthusiastic followers. God's joy and laughter are contagious.

Helen Keller was fond of saying, "Keep your face to the sunshine and you cannot see the shadow." "Happiness makes up in height for what it lacks in length" (Robert Frost). The unwise person seeks happiness in the future; the wise person grows it today. There is no sadder sight than a young Christian pessimist. Your world looks brighter from behind a smile. A smile is the shortest distance between two people.

How many people do you know who became successful doing something they hate? Author Harvey Mackay advises, "Find something you love to do and you'll never have to work another day in your life." Thomas Carlisle said, "Give me a man who sings at his work." That's the kind of person I want to hire and do business with!

Happiness is always an inside job. Our first choice should be to rejoice, knowing "that all that happens to us is working for our good if we love God and are fitting into his plans" (Rom. 8:28 TLB). "Happy is that people, whose God is the LORD" (Ps. 144:15).

Greet the unseen with cheer, not fear. "Laughter is a form of internal jogging. It moves your internal organs around. It enhances respiration. It is an igniter of great expectations" (Norman Cousins). God says in His Word, "If you don't praise Me, the rocks will" (see Luke 19:40). Let's not be replaced by a bunch of rocks!

For every minute you're angry, you lose sixty seconds of happiness. Two things contribute to happiness: what we can do without and what we can do with. People are about as happy as they've made up their minds to be. Happiness can never be found, because it was never lost.

One seldom meets a person who fails at doing what he or she likes to do. Don't worry about the job you don't like— someone else will soon have it. There is only one way to improve one's work—love it. Be like the steam kettle! Though up to its neck in hot water, it continues to sing.

🍎 Smile, it adds to your face value.

PART 3

Looking upward

If you pluck the blossoms, you must do without the fruit

■

God is a God of seasons. The Bible tells us, "To everything there is a season, and a time to every purpose under the heaven" (Eccles. 3:1). Distinctly different things happen during different seasons.

God is a God of wintertime. Winter is a season of preparation, revelation, and direction. It's also the time when roots grow. God wants to establish the right foundation in you during this season. There is no harvest in winter.

God is a God of springtime. It's a time of planting, hoeing, and nurturing. In other words, hard work. God wants you to work your plan. There's no harvest in springtime.

God is a God of summertime. Summer is a time of great growth. Now is the time when activity, interest, and people begin to surround your God-given idea. For all the activity of summer, there's only a minimal harvest. Then comes autumn.

Autumn . . . this is God's harvest time. During this season the harvest is reaped in much greater proportion than the work or activity expended. But most people never make it to the fall. Often they end up quitting along the way because they don't know what season they're in.

Your success has little to do with speed but much to do with timing and direction. What benefit is running if you're on the wrong road? The key is doing the right thing at the right time. Tryon Edwards said, "Have a time and place for everything, and do everything in its time and place and you will not only accomplish more, but have far more leisure than those who are always hurrying."

God did not create hurry. Lord Chesterfield said, "Whoever is in a hurry shows that the thing he is about is too big for him." When you are outside of the right timing, you will sow hurry and reap frustration. There is simply more to life than increasing its speed. People that hurry through life get to the end of it quicker.

When you understand that God is a God of seasons, you will be prepared to do the right thing at the right time. You will be inspired to persevere into the autumn season. God's Word is true when it says, "Let us not become weary in doing good, for at the proper time we will reap a harvest if we do not give up" (Gal. 6:9 NIV).

🍎 **Stay in season with God.**

One action is more valuable than a thousand good intentions

Few dreams come true by themselves. The test of a person lies in action. No one ever stumbled onto something big while sitting down. Even a mosquito doesn't get a slap on the back until it starts to work. A famous anonymous poem states,

> Sitting still and wishing makes no person great,
> The good Lord sends the fishing, but you must dig
> the bait.

"As [Jesus] was speaking, a woman in the crowd called out, 'God bless your mother—the womb from which you came, and the breasts that gave you suck!' He replied, 'Yes, but even more blessed are all who hear the Word of God and put it into practice'" (Luke 11:27 TLB). A doer of God's Word is even more blessed than the mother of Jesus.

Realize nothing is learned while you talk. Words without actions are the assassins of dreams. The smallest good deed is better than the greatest intention. History is made whenever you take the right action. Action is the proper fruit of knowledge. Getting an idea should be like sitting on a tack: it should make you jump up and do something.

"Go to the ant, thou sluggard; consider her ways, and be wise: which having no guide, overseer, or ruler, provideth her meat in the summer, and gathereth her food in the harvest" (Prov. 6:6–8). Nothing preaches better than an ant, even though it says nothing. You earn respect by action; inaction earns disrespect.

You should hunt for the good points in people. Remember, they have to do the same in your case . . . so do something to help them.

A middle-aged man found himself in front of the pearly gates. St. Peter explained that it's not so easy to get into heaven. There are some criteria before entry is allowed.

St. Peter asked if the man was religious in life. Did he attend church? The man answered, "No." St. Peter told him that was bad.

Was he generous? Did he give money to the poor or to charities? Again the answer was "No." St. Peter told him that was not good.

Did he do any good deeds? Help his neighbor? Anything? Still, his answer was "No." St. Peter was becoming concerned.

Exasperated, Peter said, "Look, everybody does something nice sometime. Work with me, I'm trying to help. Now think!"

The man paused and said, "There was this old lady. I came out of a store and found her surrounded by a dozen Hell's Angels. They had taken her purse and were shoving her around, taunting and cursing her.

"I got so mad I threw my bags down, fought through the crowd, and got her purse back. I helped her to her feet. I then went up to the biggest, baddest biker and told him how despicable, cowardly, and mean he was and then spat in his face."

"Wow!" said Peter. "That's impressive. When did this happen?"

"Oh, about two minutes ago," replied the man.

Some people find life an empty dream because they put nothing into it. Every time one person expresses an idea, you can find ten others who thought of it before—but took no action. Mark Twain once said, "Thunder is good, thunder is impressive, but it is lightning that does the work." The test of this book is not the reader saying "What an inspiring book!" but "I will do something!"

The devil is willing for you to confess faith as long as you don't practice it. When praying, we must simultaneously be willing to take the action God directs in the answer to our prayer. The answers to your prayers will include action. Action is attached to answers and miracles.

The Bible tells us action gives life to our faith (see James 2:26). "Even a child is known by his doings" (Prov. 20:11). Many churchgoers are singing "Standing on the Promises" when all they are doing is sitting on the premises. Too many people carefully avoid discovering the secret of success because deep down they suspect the secret may be hard work.

🍎 **Act now on God's direction.**

Adopt the pace of God

■

God is a planner, a strategist. He is perfectly organized, has a definite flow and pace. God is more like a marathon runner than a sprinter. He has our whole lives in mind, not just tomorrow. Remember, God is never late. Never try to hurry God. "He that believeth shall not make haste" (Isa. 28:16). Urgent matters are seldom urgent. Pressure usually accompanies us when we are out of God's pace.

Proverbs 16:9 says, "We should make plans, counting on God to direct us" (TLB). And Proverbs 16:3 tells us, "Commit to the LORD whatever you do, and he will establish your plans" (NIV). Those who are lukewarm give up along the way, and cowards never even start. God is the original's hope but the copy's excuse. Is God your hope or your excuse?

Adopt the pace of God. His secret is patience. There's no time lost in waiting if you're waiting on the Lord . . . and He's worth your time. The road to success runs uphill, so don't expect to break any speed records. All great achievements require time. Happiness is a direction, not a destination.

During the darkest hours of the Civil War, Abraham Lincoln responded to the question of whether he was sure God was on the North's side: "I do not know: I have not thought about that. But I am very anxious to know whether we are on God's side." Lincoln's contemporary, Henry Ward Beecher, once said, "The strength of a man consists in finding out the way God is going, and going that way."

Walking at God's pace helps establish you on the proper foundation. Nothing is permanent unless built on God's will and Word. "Except the LORD build the house, they labor in vain that build it" (Ps. 127:1). "The steps of a good man are ordered by the LORD: and he delighteth in his way" (Ps. 37:23). Never remain where God has not sent you. When God shuts and bolts the door, don't try to get in through the window.

A Christian walking in God's pace is like a candle—it must keep cool and burn at the same time. (But if you burn the candle at both ends, you're not as bright as you think.)

Every great person first learned how to obey, whom to obey, and when to obey.

> The place I choose, or place I shun,
> My soul is satisfied with none;
> But when Thy will directs my way,
> Tis equal joy to go or stay.
> Anonymous

🍎 **God has your whole life in mind when He directs you.**

The alphabet for originality

■

A Attitude	N Nonconformity
B Belief	O Objectives
C Character	P Pray
D Decisive	Q Quiet time
E Effort	R Responsibility
F Fearless	S Sensitivity
G Gratitude	T Tenacity
H Honesty	U Unhesitating
I Ideas	V Vigilant
J Joy	W Wholehearted
K Kindhearted	X E(x)ceptional
L Leadership	Y Yielded
M Merciful	Z Zealous

🍎 **From A to Z are the ways you are unique.**

In the race for excellence, there is no finish line

■

Commit yourself to excellence from the start. No legacy is as rich as excellence. The quality of your life will be in direct proportion to your commitment to excellence, regardless of what you choose to do.

> It's a fun thing about life; if you refuse to accept anything but the best, you very often get it.
>
> Somerset Maugham

It takes less time to do something right than it does to explain why you did it wrong. According to Orison Swett Marden, "There is an infinite difference between a little wrong and just right, between fairly good and the best, between mediocrity and superiority." Every day you should ask yourself: Why should my boss/client hire me instead of someone else? Why should people do business with me instead of my competitors?

> Watch your actions; they become habits. Watch your habits; they become character. Watch your character; it becomes your destiny.

> Frank Outlaw

Oliver Wendell Holmes once said, "Sin has many tools, but a lie is the handle that fits them all." Those who are given to telling white lies soon become color blind. You may go to the ends of the earth by lying, but you'll never get back. A lie has no legs to support itself—it requires other lies. When you stretch the truth, watch out for the snap back. Each time you lie, even just a little white lie, you push yourself toward failure. There is no right way to do the wrong thing. Each time you're honest you propel yourself toward greater success.

Reputation grows like a mushroom; character grows like an oak tree. A thing done right means less trouble tomorrow. Beware of a half-truth; you may get hold of the wrong half. Only you can damage your character. People of genius are admired; people of wealth are envied; people of power are feared; but only people of character are trusted.

Outside forces don't control your character. You do. The measure of your real character is what you would do if you knew you would never be found out. Be more concerned with your character than with your reputation, because your character is what you really are while your reputation is merely what others think you are.

> He that is good will infallibly become better, and he that is bad, will as certainly become worse; for vice, virtue and time are three things that never stand still.

> Charles Caleb Colton

Excellence can be attained if you . . .
Care more than others think is wise.
Risk more than others think is safe.
Dream more than others think is practical.
Expect more than others think is possible.

Anonymous

🍎 **Excellence—it's contagious. Start an epidemic!**

Is God finished with you yet?

■

If you're still breathing, the answer is no. Don't die until you're dead. Psalm 138:8 says, "The LORD will perfect that which concerneth me." God is continually perfecting and fine-tuning each of us. He wants to fulfill all of His promises and purposes in our lives.

Romans 11:29 says, "For God's gifts and his call are irrevocable" (NIV). What God has put in you stays your whole life. He still wants to use what He's given in order to fulfill His plan for your life. If you've done nothing with what He's put inside of you . . . He still wants to use you! If you've failed many times . . . He still wants to use you! How do you move again with God? Say this simple prayer: "Lord, send small opportunities into my life so I can begin to use what You've put inside of me."

Ralph Waldo Emerson said, "The creation of a thousand forests is in one acorn." The accomplishment of your destiny is held in the seeds of your God-given gifts and calling.

God begins with a positive and ends with a positive. "Being confident of this very thing, that he which hath begun a good work in you will perform it until the day of Jesus Christ" (Phil. 1:6). Jesus hasn't come back, so that means God isn't finished with you. God's will for us is momentum, building from one good work to another.

Don't just go on to other things, go on to higher things. The pains of being a Christian are all growing pains, and those growing pains lead to maturity. God's way becomes plain as we walk in it. When faith is stretched, it grows. "The more we do, the more we can do" (William Hazlitt).

Greater opportunity and momentum is the reward of past accomplishment. If you're going to climb, you've got to grab the branches, not the blossoms. Success makes failures out of too many people when they stop after a victory. Don't quit. Don't stop after a victory. When you do what you can, God will do what you can't. He's not finished with you!

🍎 **What you thought was dead still has life.**

Believe six impossible things before breakfast

■

Imagine beginning tomorrow as you have never done before. Instead of stretching your body when you get out of bed, stretch your being with all the good things God has in store for you. Think, plan, believe, and pray for things that require God's involvement.

Grab hold of each day from the start. Most people lose an hour at the beginning of the day and spend the rest of the day trying to recapture it. The first hour of the morning is the rudder of the day. Never begin your day in neutral. Create a habit of initiative. It's the person who doesn't need a boss that's usually selected to be one. When you're a self-starter, others don't have to be a crank.

Duties delayed are the devil's delight. The devil doesn't care what your plans are as long as you don't do anything about them.

It was the day after Christmas at a church in San Francisco. The pastor of the church was looking over the nativity scene when he noticed that the baby Jesus was missing from among the figures. Immediately, he turned and went outside and saw a little boy with a red wagon. In the wagon was the missing figure of Jesus.

So he walked up to the boy and said, "Well, where did you get him, my fine friend?"

The little boy replied, "I got him from the church."

"And why did you take him?"

The boy said, "Well, about a week before Christmas I prayed to the little Lord Jesus and I told him if he would bring me a red wagon for Christmas I would give him a ride around the block in it."

You will never gain what you are unwilling to go after. If you have a goal in life that requires a lot of energy, incurs a great deal of interest, and challenges you, you'll always look forward to waking up to see what the new day brings. Take the offensive; never meet trouble halfway. Your personal growth is hidden in your daily approach to life.

Seize your destiny. Don't let it slip away. If God has called you, don't look over your shoulder to see who's coming after you. "Let every man abide in the same calling wherein he was called" (1 Cor. 7:20).

"The crude and physical agony of the Cross was nothing compared to the indifference of the crowd on Main Street as Jesus passed by" (Allan Knight Chalmers). Don't live an indifferent life as if Jesus did nothing for you.

Satan trembles when he sees even the weakest Christian on his knees. Jesus is worth your time. It's what you do when you have nothing to do that reveals what you are and what you really believe. The breakfast of champions isn't Wheaties; it's connecting with God to start your day. Bring God on the scene from the start and you'll always finish strong.

🍎 Start your day right and never look back.

You'll always be more convinced by what you've discovered than by what others have found

Go from being dependent on others to being dependent on God. He is the source of your direction. Too many people base what they believe, do, and say on what other people believe, do, and say. Revelation is only revelation when it's *your* revelation. God is best known by revelation, not explanation.

Obviously, God uses ministers, Christian leaders, books, audio, video, music, and television to speak truth into our lives. But it's not enough that what they say is right. Our faith only works when we believe it for ourselves and place a demand on it. If another person's faith can't get you to heaven, it can't get you to your destiny either.

Don't believe something just because "brother so-and-so" believes. Believe because God has shown it to *you* and confirmed it in His Word. He desires a personal relationship with you. People who don't pray are really declaring they don't need God. Judas heard all Christ's sermons, but he obviously didn't allow them to become opportunities for personal revelation and discovery.

There are two kinds of unwise people. One says, "This is old, therefore it's good." The other says, "This is new, therefore it's better." Don't attempt to do something unless you're sure of it yourself; but don't abandon it simply because someone else isn't sure of you. This is shown in Jesus's response when Peter declared, "You are the Christ, the Son of the living God." Jesus told Peter, "This was not revealed to you by flesh and blood, but by my Father in heaven" (Matt. 16:17 NIV).

The most important convictions in our lives can't really be reached on the word of another. The fact is, "The Bible is so simple you have to have someone else help you misunderstand it" (Charles Capps). Theologians are always trying to make the Bible into a book without common sense. God made it easy for us to find out for ourselves.

Ask for His help. Have you ever prayed this prayer?

DEAR LORD . . . So far today, God, I've done all right. I haven't gossiped; I haven't lost my temper; I haven't been grumpy, greedy, nasty, selfish, or self-indulgent.

I'm very thankful for that. But in a few minutes, God, I'm going to get out of bed . . . and from then on, I'm going to need a lot of help.

John Wesley said it best: "When I was young I was sure of everything; in a few years, having been mistaken a thousand times, I was not half so sure of most things as I was before; at present, I am hardly sure of anything but what God has revealed to me."

🍎 Go from knowing what others believe to knowing what you believe.

Something dominates everyone's day

What influences, dominates, and controls your day? Is it the daily news, your noisy negative neighbor, the memory of a failure? Or is it God's plan for you, His Word in your heart, a song of praise to Him? Let the plan God has for your life dominate your day . . . or something else will.

Mediocrity has its own type of intensity. It wants to dominate your day. It starts somewhere and leads to everywhere. It can influence and affect every area of your life if you let it. "Some temptations come to the industrious, but all temptations attack the idle" (Charles Spurgeon).

A fruitful life is not the result of chance. It's the result of right choices. If the bad things in life can try to dominate your day, then so much more can the good things.

When the news tries to dominate your day, let the Good News dominate your day.

When the past tries to dominate your day, let your dreams dominate your day.

When fear tries to dominate your day, let right action dominate your day.

When procrastination tries to dominate your day, let small steps dominate your day.

When wrong influences try to dominate your day, let right associations dominate your day.

When confusion tries to dominate your day, let God's Word dominate your day.

When loneliness tries to dominate your day, let prayer dominate your day.

When strife tries to dominate your day, let peace dominate your day.

When your mind tries to dominate your day, let the Holy Spirit dominate your day.

When envy tries to dominate your day, let blessing others dominate your day.

When greed tries to dominate your day, let giving dominate your day.

❦ Let God dominate your day.

Once you've found a better way, make that way better

All progress is due to those who weren't satisfied to let well enough alone. "Acorns were good until bread was found" (Francis Bacon). The majority of people meet with failure because they lack persistence in creating new plans to add to those that succeed.

If at first you do succeed, try something harder. There's no mistake as great as the mistake of not going on after a victory. If you can't think up a new idea, find a way to make better use of an old one. "Where we cannot invent, we may at least improve" (Charles Caleb Colton).

Don't look for *the* answer to your problem; look for *many* answers, then choose the best one. The person who succeeds is the one who does more than is necessary—and continues doing it. As Zig Ziglar says, "The difference between ordinary and extraordinary is that little extra."

There's always a way, and there's always a better way. When you've found something—look again. School is never out! The more you truly desire something, the more you will try to find a better way.

The deeper we go in God, the deeper He goes in us. "A wise man will hear, and will increase learning" (Prov. 1:5). If you're satisfied with what's good, you'll never have what's best.

"It's what you learn after you know it all that counts" (John Wooden). The man who thinks he knows it all has merely stopped thinking. If you think you've arrived, you'll be left behind. The important thing is this: to be able at any moment to sacrifice what we are for what we could become. A successful person continues to look for work even after he has found a job.

Cause something to happen. Thomas Edison said, "Show me a thoroughly satisfied man, I will show you a failure." "There are two kinds of men who never amount to very much," Cyrus H. K. Curtis remarked one day to his associate, Edward Bok. "And what kinds are those?" inquired Bok. "Those who cannot do what they are told," replied the famous publisher, "and those who can do nothing else." Find a better way and make that better.

🍎 **God always has a better way.**

God made you

■

God made you different, not indifferent.
God made you extraordinary, not ordinary.
God made you significant, not insignificant.
God made you competent, not incompetent.
God made you active, not passive.
God made you indispensable, not dispensable.
God made you effective, not defective.
God made you adept, not inept.
God made you distinct, not nebulous.
God made you adequate, not inadequate.
God made you efficient, not inefficient.
God made you superior, not inferior.
God made you responsible, not irresponsible.
God made you solvent, not insolvent.
God made you sane, not insane.

God made you efficient, not deficient.
God made you consistent, not inconsistent.
God made you insightful, not despiteful.
God made you irresistible, not resistible.
God made you sensitive, not insensitive.
God made you uncommon, not common.
God made you decisive, not indecisive.
God made you an original, not a copy.

When God put you together it put a smile on His face; it pleased Him according to 1 Corinthians 12. Accept the way He made you and the unique plan He has for your life. His plans are good in every way. As Ethel Waters said, "I know I'm somebody, 'cause God don't make no junk."

🍎 Be yourself—who else is better qualified?

The worst buy is an alibi

■

Excuses are the nails used to build a house of failure. An alibi is worse than a lie, for an alibi is a lie guarded. Alibis are egotism wrong side out. George Washington Carver observed, "Ninety-nine percent of the failures come from people who have the habit of making excuses."

When you're good at making excuses, it's hard to excel at anything else. Don't make excuses, make progress. Excuses always replace progress. You may fail many times, but you aren't a failure until you blame somebody or something else.

There may be many reasons for failure, but there is not a single excuse. Never let a challenge become your alibi. You have a choice: you can let the obstacle be an alibi or you can take it as an opportunity. No alibi will ever serve the purpose of God.

Those who are unfaithful will always find an alibi. "I never knew a man who was good at making excuses who was good at anything else" (Ben Franklin). Quitting and failure always begin with alibis, justification, pity trips, and feeling sorry for yourself. The person who really wants to do something finds a way where others find excuses.

At a recent seminar, one of the speakers began his presentation with what was initially considered a confrontational remark. He paused very dramatically and said, "What lies do you keep telling yourself?"

Although the room fell deathly silent, everyone knew his question deeply touched a nerve. He could just as easily have said, "What alibis do you keep telling yourself?"

In life you can have results or reasons. If you are not getting the results you want, the reasons are the lies you keep telling yourself. Lies and alibis create the false idea that you're powerless to make things any different than the way they are.

Aren't we all liars in this way? We love our excuses and go to extreme lengths to hold on to them. After all, our reasons are our stories, and our stories define us. Those experiences made us who we are today! It's just the way things are . . .

Results or reasons—which do you have more of? If you answered reasons, it's time to analyze the lies. Be careful what you agree with! The results can be lethal.

Excuses always precipitate failure. "Bread of deceit is sweet to a man; but afterwards his mouth shall be filled with gravel" (Prov. 20:17). Those who are most successful in making excuses have no energy left for anything else.

It's been said an excuse is usually a thin skin of falsehood stretched tightly over a bald-faced lie. For every sin you commit, Satan is ready to provide an excuse. By saying "The conditions are not quite right," you limit God. If you wait for the conditions to be perfect you will never obey Him.

Success is a matter of luck. Ask any failure. There are always enough excuses available if you are weak enough to use them. Don't buy that alibi.

🍎 Exchange your alibis for opportunities.

The doors of opportunity are marked "push"

■

Get aggressive and go after opportunities. Otherwise, they may not find you. The reason some people don't go very far in life is because they sidestep opportunity and shake hands with procrastination. Procrastination is the grave in which opportunity is buried. When opportunity knocks at your front door, don't be caught out in the backyard looking for four-leaf clovers. For the tenacious person there is always time and opportunity.

Watch for big problems; they disguise big opportunities. Opposition, distraction, and challenges always surround the birth of a dream. So make the most of all that comes and the least of all that goes. Adversity is fertile soil for creativity.

To the alert Christian, interruptions are divinely inserted opportunities. If you're looking for a big opportunity, look

for a big problem. Turn the tables on adversity. Adversity has advantages.

Life's disappointments are opportunity's hidden appointments. When God is going to do something wonderful, He begins with difficulty; when He's going to do something very wonderful, He begins with impossibility!

Francis Bacon said, "A wise man will make more opportunities than he finds." It's more valuable to find a situation that redistributes opportunity than one that redistributes wealth. Have you ever noticed that great people are never lacking for opportunities? When highly successful people are interviewed, they always mention their big plans for the future. Most of us would think, "If I were in their shoes, I'd kick back and do nothing." Success doesn't diminish their dreams. They've always been that way, even before they were great.

There's far more opportunity than ability. Life's full of golden opportunities for doing what we're called to do. Start with what you can do; don't stop because of what you can't do. In the orchard of opportunity, it is better to pick the fruit than to wait for it to fall in your lap.

Greater opportunities and joy come to those who make the most of small opportunities. In the parable of the talents the master told the servant who used what he had, "Well done, good and faithful servant; thou hast been faithful over a few things, I will make thee ruler over many things: enter thou into the joy of thy Lord" (Matt. 25:23).

Many people seem to think opportunity means a chance to get money without earning it. God's best gifts to us are not things but opportunities. And those doors of opportunity are marked "Push."

🍎 Opportunity is all around you.

Nugget #47

Expand your horizons

■

We all live under the same sky, but we don't have the same horizon. Originals always see a bigger picture. Expanding your horizons means being able to see the greater potential all around you. When you expand your horizons, your life will change. You will begin to see things around you very differently.

The world's demands don't control the Christian's supply. Do you risk enough to exercise your faith? "Aim at the sun and you may not reach it, but your arrow will fly far higher than if aimed at an object on a level with yourself" (Joel Hawes).

A woman's horizons were changed forever when she came up to Picasso in a restaurant and asked him to scribble something on her napkin. She said she'd be happy to pay him whatever he felt it was worth. Picasso did what she asked and then said, "That will be $10,000."

"But you did that in only thirty seconds," the woman said.

"No," Picasso replied. "It has taken me forty years to do that."

"If the Son [of God] therefore shall make you free, ye shall be free indeed" (John 8:36). Knowing Jesus brings freedom, and freedom releases you to think higher and see farther. Vision is the art of seeing things that are unseen.

If what you did yesterday still looks big to you, you haven't done much today. You'll never learn faith in comfortable surroundings. When God stretches you, you never come back to your original shape. A person who's afraid of doing too much always does too little. Make sure the road you're on is not leading to a cul-de-sac.

Someone once said, "Man cannot discover new oceans unless he has courage to lose sight of the shore." That's why I believe Jesus wants us to "Launch out to the deep" (Luke 5:4). Enough spiritual power is going to waste to put Niagara Falls to shame. Unless you try to do something beyond what you have already done and mastered, you will never grow.

🍎 **Look around . . . then look a little farther . . . then look a little farther still.**

Good intentions aren't good enough

■

You can't test your destiny cautiously. "Don't play for safety—it's the most dangerous thing in the world" (Hugh Walpole). How many national championship football teams run a quarterback sneak on every play?

The key is this: reject the safety of staying where you are for the amazement of what you could become. Unless you attempt to do something beyond what you have already done, you'll never grow.

I've seen a lot while traveling across the United States and around the world over the past twenty years. Sometimes I find myself going back to the same places and seeing the same people, with years separating the visits. Often the change in appearances is startling (I'm glad I've not aged either). Sometimes it's not (lucky people). Every once in a while I meet with someone stuck in exactly the same place as the last time I saw them. It's like they're in a time warp. Same problem, same excuses. Same story, same "no ending." And here's an absolute: they're always unhappy. There's a reason why. They are doing, acting, and being the same year after year. No wonder they're miserable and sad.

Mediocrity can be defined as the best of the worst, and the worst of the best. Potential is the emptiest word in the world. It means you haven't done your best yet. Good intentions are like checks drawn on a bank where you have no account. Every mediocre person has good intentions.

It's been said the biggest enemy of great is good. Don't accept good as good enough. Tolerating mediocrity in others makes you more mediocre. Only an average person is always at his best.

You can't make a place for yourself in the sun if you keep taking refuge under the family tree. Go! Launch out! "People who never do any more than they get paid for, never get paid for any more than they do" (Elbert Hubbard). It's simple. Do more . . .

An overcautious person burns bridges of opportunity before ever coming to them. Most of the people who sit around and wait for the harvest haven't planted anything. The average person doesn't want much and usually gets less than that.

One bold action is more valuable than a thousand good intentions.

❦ Go from good intentions to great beginnings.

Don't miss the silver lining only looking for the gold

■

Jesus never taught people how to make a living. He taught people how to live. "God doesn't call us to be successful. He calls us to be faithful" (Albert Hubbard). Most people have their eye on the wrong goals. Is your goal more money, a higher position, or more influence? These are not goals, but rather by-products of goals.

Having the proper perspective is critical.

What's a true goal? It's this: "Keep this Book of the Law always on your lips; meditate on it day and night, so that you may be careful to do everything written in it. Then you will be prosperous and successful" (Josh. 1:8 NIV). Work to *become*, not *acquire*. God wants eternal fruit, not religious nuts.

Do not seek success in and of itself. Instead, seek the truth and you'll find both. "But seek ye first the kingdom of God, and his righteousness; and all these things shall be added unto you" (Matt. 6:33). Measure wealth not by the things you have, but by the things you have for which you would not take money.

"Happiness is not a reward—it is a consequence. Suffering is not a punishment—it is a result" (Robert Green Ingersoll). Do the very best you can and leave the results to God. Potential is the most empty word in the world, but God can fill it to overflowing.

"Oh how small a portion of earth will keep us when we're dead, who ambitiously seek after the whole world while we are living" (anonymous). "For what shall it profit a man, if he shall gain the whole world, and lose his own soul?" (Mark 8:36). People are funny: they spend money they don't have, to buy things they don't need, to impress people they don't like. Don't spend your life unproductively like Frank Perkins of Los Angeles. In 1992 he made an attempt on the world record for flagpole sitting. By the time he had come down, eight hours short of the four-hundred-day record, his sponsor had gone bust, his girlfriend had left him, and his phone and electricity had been cut off.

Success lies not in achieving what you aim at, but in aiming at what you ought to achieve. Do what God wants you to do, and trust Him to take care of the rest.

❦ Seek God first and all you'll really want will find you.

Invest in yourself

God regularly sends us divine opportunities for investment in ourselves. Be on the lookout for them. He does this first through His Word, which is the best investment we can put into ourselves. But He also sends many other "investment opportunities" to us. In my own life, I've incorporated many of these. For example, my wife and I have a weekly date night that has been a great investment in our marriage. Also, every Saturday when the kids were little we would "sneak out" on Mom to have an early breakfast together. This time was great for the kids and me, while allowing my wife a nice quiet break.

Everything you say or do creates an investment somewhere. Whether that investment generates a dividend or a loss depends on you. Always do your best, for what you plant now you will harvest later.

One of the biggest mistakes you can make is to believe you work for someone else. No matter how many bosses you appear to have, you really work for the Lord. You can't look to others as your source. That's why tapping into God's investment opportunities is so important. They are His way of developing and instructing us. When an archer misses the mark, he turns and looks for the fault within himself. Failure to hit the bull's-eye is never the fault of the target. "To improve your aim—improve yourself" (Gilbert Arland).

When prosperity comes, don't spend it all; give some back to others and make an investment in yourself. Half of knowing what you want is knowing what you must give up before you get it. Time invested in improving ourselves cuts down on time wasted in disapproving others.

"Study to show thyself approved unto God, a workman that needeth not to be ashamed" (2 Tim. 2:15). Investment doesn't cost, it pays. You cannot fulfill your destiny without applying the principle of investing in yourself.

🍎 **Seize the opportunities God sends to invest in yourself.**

Expect the opposite

■

One of the major reasons the Bible was written was to teach us to expect the opposite of what we see in the world. Indeed, "I can't believe my eyes" is a very spiritual statement, for we are called to walk by faith and not by sight. God tells us we must give to receive, die to live, and serve to lead.

One of God's principles of opposites is found in John 3:30: "He [Jesus] must increase, but I must decrease." In this world of opposites—what Pat Robertson calls "the upside-down kingdom"—"He who goes to and fro weeping . . . shall indeed come again with a shout of joy" (Ps. 126:6 NASB), and "He that loseth his life for my [Jesus's] sake shall find it" (Matt. 10:39).

When fear comes, expect the opposite—faith to rise up inside you.

When symptoms attack your body, expect the opposite—God's healing power to touch you.

When sadness tries to attach itself to you, expect the opposite—joy to flood your being.

When lack comes in, expect the opposite—God's provision to meet your needs.

When confusion comes, expect the opposite—God's peace to comfort you.

When darkness tries to cover you, expect the opposite—God's light to shine on you.

For ye see your calling, brethren, how that not many wise men after the flesh, not many mighty, not many noble, are called: But God hath chosen the foolish things of the world to confound the wise; and God hath chosen the weak things of the world to confound the things which are mighty . . . that no flesh should glory in his presence. (1 Cor. 1:26–27, 29)

God chooses ordinary men and women for extraordinary work. In the midst of your destiny, if you feel unwise and weak, fret not. God is getting ready to move on your behalf and use you. The Sermon on the Mount was preached to lift us out of the valley of discouragement.

This famous poem says it best:

> Doubt sees the obstacles
> Faith sees the way
> Doubt sees the darkest night
> Faith sees the day
> Doubt dreads to take a step
> Faith soars on high
> Doubt questions "Who believes?"
> Faith answers "I."
> > Anonymous

🍎 **Remember, looks are deceiving—especially first impressions of your problems.**

Memo/email

■

To: You
From: God
Date: Today
Re: What I think about you

I want to tell you I've known you since before the foundations of time. I even know the hairs on your head. I put you together on purpose, for a purpose. I looked at you and saw you were fearfully and wonderfully made. I even created you in My image.

I know the plans I have for you. Plans to prosper and not to harm you. Plans to give you a hope and a future.

I also gave you gifts to prepare and equip you for the plan I have for you. These gifts are irrevocable. Don't neglect them. Exercise and stir them up!

I want you to be confident about this: when I begin a good work in you, I will carry it on to completion until the day Jesus comes back.

Although you will encounter tribulations in this world, I want you to know in Me you have peace. Be of good cheer. I have overcome the world.

I am not slack concerning My promises. Forever My Word is settled in heaven and My faithfulness to all generations. When I have spoken it, I will also bring it to pass. When I've purposed it, I will also do it.

You can look to Me as a refuge and strength, a very present help in trouble. Cast your burdens upon Me and I will sustain you. I will never suffer the righteous to be moved.

Come unto Me when you labor and are heavy laden, and I will give you rest. For I am your rock, your fortress, your deliverer, your strength in whom you can trust. Though you fall you shall not be utterly cast down. I will uphold you with My hand.

Don't listen to the ungodly, don't stand with sinners, and don't sit with the scornful. But rather delight yourself all day long in My Word. If you do, you will be like a tree planted by the river. You will bring forth fruit in season, and whatever you do will prosper.

Finally, I want you to know I love you. I love you so much I gave My only Son for you. When you believe in Him you will not die but have healing, freedom, victory, forgiveness, and eternal life.

🍎 All I want is all of you.

■

A final word

Be the original person God intended you to be. Don't settle for anything less. Don't look back. Look forward and decide today to take steps toward His unique plan for your life.

What's the secret of success?

"Takes pain," said the window.

"Keep cool," said the ice.

"Don't stop," said the green light.

"Drive hard," said the hammer.

"Measure up," said the scale.

"Be up to date," said the calendar.

"Be led," said the pencil.

"Be sharp," said the knife.

"Be accountable," said the ledger.

"Be warm," said the fire.

"Be on time," said the watch.

"Stick to it," said the glue.

"Be bright," said the spotlight.

"Be an original," said the painting.

John Mason is an international bestselling author, minister, author coach, and noted speaker. He's the founder and president of Insight International and Insight Publishing Group. Both organizations are dedicated to helping people reach their dreams and fulfill their God-given destinies.

He has authored twelve books, including *An Enemy Called Average, Let Go of Whatever Makes You Stop,* and *Know Your Limits—Then Ignore Them,* which have sold over 1.4 million copies and been translated into thirty-five different languages throughout the world. His books are widely regarded as a source of godly wisdom, scriptural motivation, and practical principles. His writings have been published twice in *Reader's Digest* along with numerous other national and international publications.

Known for his quick wit, powerful thoughts, and insightful ideas, he's a popular speaker across the US and around the world.

John and his wife, Linda, have four children: Michelle, Greg, Michael, and David. They reside in Tulsa, Oklahoma.

John welcomes the opportunity to speak at your church, conference, retreat, or business organization.

Also, if you have any prayer requests, feel free to contact his office.

He can be reached at the following:

P.O. Box 54996
Tulsa, OK 74155
Phone: (918) 493-1718
Email: contact@freshword.com
www.freshword.com

Change the way you think . . . and you can change your life.

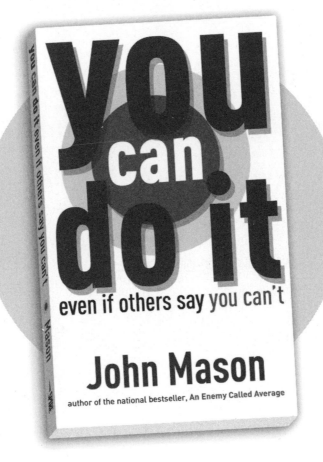

Find the inspiration for pursuing your dreams—right between these pages. You can live a fruitful and fulfilling life, believing that God will provide the means to accomplish the impossible. And the best part is—you can start right now!

Dare to be you and great things will happen!

Success in life is not an accident—but it's not just dumb luck either. If you are ready to achieve positive results in your life, then *Believe You Can!*